# Humor in School
# Is Serious Business
# (sort of)

## Why Humor Belongs in Every Classroom
## and How to Get It Into Yours

### by B. Lee Hurren, Ph.D.

Incentive Publications, Inc.
Nashville, TN

This book is dedicated to all of the great, caring teachers in the world
who bring humor, fun, excitement, and meaning into
the lives of their students.

Many thanks to:

- My wife and best friend, Susan. Thank you for supporting me in all that I do, and for sharing humor, love, and laughter at all times. Thank you to our five children (Elizabeth, Troy, Byron, Daniel, and Emma) for not acting too embarrassed by your dad's silly whimsicalitiness.

- My parents, Carolyn and Weiler, for bringing me into the world, teaching me what's right, and giving me all they had.

- Meggin McIntosh, for exemplifying and inspiring extraordinary teaching, encouraging me to write and publish, and for reviewing chapters of this book.

- Gini Cunningham, for offering valuable editorial and grammatical advice.

- Roni Jo Draper, for reviewing chapters and offering advice for readability.

- Gil Folk, for taking a chance on a young, energetic, devoted, and enthusiastic, yet unaccomplished college graduate, and offering me my first teaching job.

- Lee Chazen, for adding all the fun, excitement, comedy, and thrills while teaching.

- Troy and Cindy Jones (and children Matika, Mikaela, Mariah, and Jamison Lee), for your examples of hard work and dedication, and for maintaining positive and humorous attitudes in times of difficulty.

- My editor, Marjorie Frank, and everyone at Incentive Publications, for taking a chance on this book and helping me through the process.

- All of my former and current students, for your willingness to share humor with me in the educational process.

Cartoons by Addison
Cover design and book design by Mary Bullock
Additional Artwork by Kathleen Bullock
Edited by Marjorie Frank

ISBN 978-0-86530-254-9

2   3   4   5   6   7   8   9   10                13   12

Printed by Sheridan Books, Inc., Chelsea, Michigan • August 2012
www.incentivepublications.com

# Contents

# 2 Why Chapter 2 Comes Before Chapter 1 and Why I Wrote This Book and Why You Should Read It

*"On a positive note, I did enjoy 23 of the words you used."*

Don't be alarmed. You didn't buy a book with the first chapter missing. I just happen to like Chapter 2 better than Chapter 1, so I'm putting Chapter 2 first. Also, it gives you a little boost on your reading. You can buy the book and immediately say to the checkout clerk, "I'm already on Chapter 2 . . . I love this book."

**I wrote this book for many reasons. Here's the first:** A few years ago at an international education conference, I heard someone say, "You must write a book." Now, I'm not going to lie to you this early in the effort. (That will come later.) So let me confess that there is the smallest of chances (teeny, tiny, actually) that the comment "You must write a book" was perhaps not directed to me. I hadn't presented anything at the conference yet (so it wasn't as if the person knew whether or not I had any good ideas), and the person called me "Steve."

But I wasn't wearing a name tag and, I must admit, I do kind of look like a Steve. I was in an area where a lot of people were flocking around a presenter from Stanford University named Steve something, but he wasn't wearing a name tag either, so we're even as far as that goes. In fact, I look more like a Steve than he does.

When I saw the crowd, I assumed that there must be a buffet at the front, or at least hors d'oeuvres, so I fell in line with the mob in hopes of finding some free snackage. While clutching a napkin and empty plate, I got lost in contemplation, calculating how many custard-filled éclairs I could courteously devour. Suddenly, I found myself facing not a dessert buffet, but the prestigious orator from Stanford. About 150 people were staring at me as the clamor and babble turned to suffocating silence. I might have been wearing a bib, too. I don't remember.

Dr. Whoever from Stanford looked into my eyes and said these four words that I'll never forget, "What do you want?" It's not just **what** he said that made the event so memorable, but **how** he said those four words. He put a certain scholarly emphasis on the word "you" that helped me feel included and on an equal level. I wish that you could have been there to experience it.

After that critical inquiry, he turned to his adoring flock for immediate approval. I felt all tingly, nervous, and speechless. Yet I knew that I must answer the academic's question. So I uttered, "pastries," and lowered my head to leave with about fifteen of my **own** newly found admirers, or possibly just hungry people looking for eats. As I turned to depart, discussion around the Stanford dude started again and I thought I (sort of) distinctly heard someone say, "Steve, you must write a book." I stopped in my tracks and said to myself,

*"No problem. People are always confusing me with Steve."*

"Yes, I must. But don't call me Steve." To this day I don't know for certain whether or not that comment was addressed to me (for the way I handled the Stanford scholar's question) or to someone else. Either way, I was sure that a book had just become part of my destiny.

**The second reason I wrote this book** is that I thought it would be fun. I was wrong. I have enjoyed writing very few words of this book—like maybe twenty-three, total. I don't recommend writing a book. In fact, I recommend **not** writing a book. Writing a book is a terrible process. After enduring the arduous and wearisome task, I must say I am surprised that there are more than seventeen people who have written books—ever. Reading a book is much more enjoyable than writing one. The thinking takes forever; the writing takes forever; the typing takes forever; the editing and re-editing takes forever. And then, when you finally allow some people to read it (people who have been begging you to read this all-consuming achievement that has caused you to sweat, bleed (paper cut), and cry, they say, "Yeah, it's okay, I guess, maybe, no yeah, it's, you know, good."

**Reason number three for writing this book** is that I thought it might be lucrative. Since I'm still being completely honest here in Chapter 1 (well, actually Chapter 2 posing as Chapter 1), yes, I thought it would be awesome to make a bunch of extra money from writing a great book. But reality has now set in: this book will never be declared great. I'm now hoping for an honorable review of "mediocre." With the amount of time I have spent on this book, I could've made more money cleaning animal cages for tips at the local pound.

*"I'm writing a book."*

**Here's reason number four:** I really thought it would be self-fulfilling to write and publish a book. And it was—filling of **myself**. While writing, wondering what to write, pretending to my friends and relatives that I was writing, and playing Nerf basketball in my office to avoid writing, I filled myself with every kind of snack food known to humans.

**Reason number five**, quite simply, is that I'm a lunatic. Let's go back to the first reason that I wrote this book (the incident where someone possibly might have said to me, "You must write a book"). When I was a kid (my whole life up until last week), my dad often asked me, "Do you do everything that people say to do? If someone said you should jump off that cliff, would you do it?"

*Note to reader: I grew up near Charleston, South Carolina. There are not many cliffs there. I remember looking around a lot and thinking two things: A) "What cliff?" and B) "It depends on how high the cliff is and what's at the bottom."*

*Another note to reader: I **did** jump off a cliff one time, and I took a horse with me. I was working on my horsemanship merit badge in Boy Scouts and I walked my horse right off a cliff.*

So I guess that my answer to the original question is "Yes." But my point is this: I should've thought things through a little better and that way I wouldn't have maimed a rental horse, hurt my leg, tried to write a book, and a lot of other unintelligent things (like going over a waterfall—backwards).

**My last reason for writing this book** is, I hope, a little more useful to you. Over the past twenty years, many students have asked me questions such as:

- If teachers hate **children** so much, then why did they become teachers?

- If teachers hate **people** so much, then why did they become teachers?

- If teachers hate **students** so much, then why did they become teachers?

- Why are so many teachers so grumpy?

I love teaching and associating with today's youth. I want students everywhere to experience fun and excitement in the classroom while they learn—and not to feel as if their teachers are stuffy or mean. I want them to spend their time in a low-stress climate that has the absolute best possible conditions for their brains to engage with ideas. So how can I do this? I believe that one of the best ways to spread the message is to publish a book and hope that teachers, administrators, coaches, school staff, politicians, parents, guardians, grandparents, great-grandparents, not-so-great grandparents, bankers, movie ticket-takers, pet food tasters, and Himalayan guides will read it and use some of the information from it.

I'm going to get sort of serious about this now. The purpose of this book is to demonstrate that teachers everywhere can effectively incorporate humor into the classroom without being natural comedians or clowns. Teaching and learning don't have to be funny, but they can and should be fun. The presence of laughter in the classroom is not necessarily a sign of goofing off; instead, it demonstrates that students are paying attention to what is going on around them. Humor in the school keeps the learning process from becoming dull and boring. At the same time, it stimulates the brain and enhances creativity, critical thinking, and understanding.

> Teachers everywhere can effectively incorporate humor into the classroom without being natural comedians or clowns.

This book reminds teachers and administrators why we became educators. It's time for school to be enjoyable; and if you are already having a good time—then have **more** fun!

Even with all of the restrictions, paperwork, and high-stakes testing, we can still teach the way we feel is best for our students. Maybe we just need to remember the delightful, creative things that can be done in the classroom. This book sets out to help recall those things, and induces laughter along the way. Buy it, read it, and then pass it on to a friend. (Or even better, buy him or her a copy to own—so that I can pocket another eleven cents.)

> All students have the right to learn in a comfortable, safe, and fun environment.

All students have the right to learn in a comfortable, safe, and fun environment. When they have this, students will be motivated to learn. They'll **want** to come to class! And if you pay attention to the growing pile of research on brain-compatible learning (and if you're smart, you will pay attention), you'll believe that humor **will** help your students

*"No, not a funeral. We're going to school."*

understand what they learn more thoroughly and remember it longer. Please join me in making this a reality. And please get serious (sort of) about the role of humor in your school.

## Chapter Summary

- My name should've been Steve.

- Writing a book is worse than giving birth, as proven by the fact that more people have given birth than have written a book.

- My dad shared many words of wisdom.

- Too bad I didn't listen.

- Teaching is fun.

- Humor belongs in every school and every classroom.

- You don't have to be a comedian to add humor to your classroom.

- Buy multiple copies of this book.

## Summary of the Summary

If my parents had named me Steve, then things would be different—maybe.

# 1

## The Case for Unsuppressed Chortles in the Academic Environment

### Introduction

It's fairly easy to find thousands of published articles and books on topics related to human emotions. The majority of these deal with fear, anger, and anxiety—while relatively little is written about positive phenomena such as humor. This book adds one more resource to the positive side, the good side, the beneficial side; okay, I'll be brash and say it—the **right** side. Maybe if authors produce more positive publications to read, we won't have so many scared, angry, and anxious people in the world.

Those who have studied humor generally agree that more research is needed on the topic in order to better understand and utilize its powerful positive potential. However, in academic circles, the study of humor has often been treated as frivolous. (Take this from a guy who tried to write a dissertation on humor and have it taken seriously!) The argument seems to be that humor is not serious; therefore, it is not possible to make a serious study of it, and anyone who attempts this probably just wants to goof off. And that is my cue to introduce myself: Hi! I'm Lee, and I like to goof off. I also like to seriously study fun topics. Just because humor and laughter are not grave, it should not be assumed that they can't be analyzed from a serious perspective. (But make no mistake; this book is only sort of serious. It has a little bit of research and seriousnesscossity, but it also includes a lot of goofing off, humor, fun, wacky stories, and maybe a few made-up words.)

Most teachers (at least the good ones) strive to attract and maintain students' attention, increase learning, inspire cognition and metacognition (two of the biggest words in my vocabulary), and limit distractions and discipline issues. Used wisely, humor in the classroom goes a long way toward taking care of all of the above. When teachers spice up the classroom with humor, students enjoy classes and learn more. If you need proof of this principle, you can read the research of McDermott and Rothenberg (2000), or you can just ask some students.

**Humor facilitates attention and motivation, improves teacher-student rapport, and helps the brain understand and retain ideas.**

Here's a nearly perfect sample question to ask: "Hey, dude (or insert student's name), do you prefer classes where teachers share humor and make learning fun, or classes that are dull and boring? (Ask 850 randomly selected students and then write 294 pages about the experience, and you will have your very own Ph.D.!)

Teachers, administrators, and other school personnel constantly search for better ways to improve students' educational experiences. It's a shame that much of that well-intentioned searching produces more high-stakes testing for the students and increased accountability for the teachers. This book is my attempt to change some of that because I am passionate about this idea: It is important—no, critical—for all teachers to have a sense of humor and share it with their students. (Be encouraged—if you don't naturally have a great sense of humor, there's hope for you. With some work and the help of this book, you can develop one!)

> Students really **do** learn more and behave better in a humor-filled environment.

Our school systems have been so concerned with standardized test scores, discipline and punishment, failure, fear, objectives, mandates such as "No Child Left Behind," more standardized test scores, benchmarks, grades and grade inflation, drugs and alcohol, dropouts, and even more standardized test scores—that our schools have become rather unpleasant, unwelcoming, undesirable, uncomfortable, unenviable, unpalatable, and uninviting places to be. In other words, attending school has become "unfun" for many students of all ages. In fact, for some students and teachers, school is so stressful that good teaching and real learning (two main objectives of schooling) are actually hindered. It is my hope that this book will help bring some of the delight and laughter back into our schools and help more students stay in school longer.

This book will show you that, when taken seriously (sort of), humor in school benefits teachers, students, and administrators. Humor facilitates attention and motivation, improves teacher-student rapport, and helps the brain understand and retain ideas. It makes all subjects more palatable to students. Learning experiences are less tedious, more creative, more satisfying, and more memorable. Students really **do** learn more and behave better in a humor-filled environment. They actually **can** maintain high academic standards while they laugh and enjoy themselves. (There's a bonus for the adults: their jobs are more satisfying and less stressful, too.)

## Chapter Summary

- In the presence of humor, students learn more, and there are fewer discipline problems.

- Humor in school helps teachers enjoy their jobs and **do** a better job.

## Summary of the Summary

Humor in school is good.

## Super Summation

Humor good.

*"Before I pass out these teacher-evaluation surveys, I'd like to remind you about that really funny 'knock-knock' joke I told last month."*

# 3

## A School Without Laughter Is Like a Cone Without Ice Cream

### The Benefits of Humor

*Note to reader: At the end of this chapter, I will give you some boring research-type information on the different benefits discussed here. Because you paid for the book (I hope), you are not obligated to read the research stuff. But it may build some character—you know, such as when you were a kid pulling weeds and you complained, "Why do I have to work in the garden when I don't even want to eat any of these vegetables?" and your mom replied, "Because it builds character."*

The most obvious benefit of including humor in the school day is this: **It makes school a more pleasant place to be**. Humor in school keeps the learning process from becoming tedious and boring. That one factor is a huge boost to effective teaching and learning. Teachers are the primary influence on classroom climate, and the "feel" of the school or classroom environment is extremely important in determining student learning. If the use of humor can positively influence the classroom climate, then humor in the classroom can have a positive effect on student achievement. Make your school a pleasant place to be, and you'll see rewards outside individual classrooms. Skillful use of humor by the school principal or other administrator promotes a more positive school climate—resulting in greater effectiveness of school-wide programs and other efforts. (Check out Chapter 17 for more humor details directed to principals.) But this is about far more than just having fun or being comfortable. The climate that includes humor yields benefits that reach into every corner of school life: academic performance, attendance, relationships (between students and adults, adults and adults, and students and students), attitudes and behaviors, and even health.

## Humor Eases Social Contact

I have heard that humor is the shortest distance between two people. However, when I shared this with my mathematician friend (who happens to use more than average amounts of humor in his classroom), he said, "No it's not. It's a straight line that is the shortest distance between people." So I spent the next two hours explaining to him what I meant. I explained that individuals who express more humor are generally considered by others to be more socially active.

He nodded his head in the affirmative and said, "Yes, but the shortest distance between any two people is still a straight line."

He started to pull out a math book to show me an example. I wanted to avoid any confrontation with a math textbook. So I quickly explained my point: "Teachers can help put their students at ease in the classroom by using humor, thus giving the learning environment a fresh, vital, and spontaneous feel. This inspires students to share answers, information, and ask questions."

"Still not as short as a straight line," he said.

As he got close to the page he wanted in the math text, I grabbed him in a headlock and squeezed as hard as I could, asking, "Don't you feel more comfortable around your principal when she uses humor in meetings and at other times in your presence? Don't you feel that teachers who use humor are more likeable than those who don't? Don't you feel that using humor in your classroom enhances your ability to connect with your students?"

As I re-gripped his head and applied the pressure a little more enthusiastically, I asked, "Don't you feel that when we use humor in conversations we talk more easily and make more eye contact?"

As I heard him say, "Ahhjjcck," I asked one last question: "Don't you think that humor is the shortest distance between two people?"

I'm almost certain that I heard him gasp something like, "Yessir" just before he passed out. However, it could have been "straight line." It was hard to tell, because he was so busy struggling to get oxygen into his lungs. We're not quite as good friends as we used to be, but I made my point: Humor nurtures positive social contact in schools. It helps students feel more at ease, and when they feel more at ease, they are more likely to participate, engage with material, and learn something.

*Humor in School is Serious Business*

## Humor Gets and Maintains Attention

Nobody wants to be left out of a joke. When I first went to Chile at age 19, I had studied Spanish for only two months. For the first six weeks, I was confused and speechless, but it didn't really bother me. People could point at me and stare with pitiful, sad looks on their faces while talking about me. Or they could point and kick dirt on me while saying words like, "estúpido, idiota, gringo tonto, torpe, necio, imbécil, insano, and lunático," but I just didn't care. People could tell tremendously exciting stories with great animation, and this just wouldn't get my attention. Actually, the previous two sentences are complete lies. The people of Chile were always incredibly kind and caring, and I love a good story. But during those first few weeks in Chile, I never really ached to know what was being discussed—until someone laughed. Then I just had to know. I demanded an explanation. I could not stand to be left out of something funny.

> **Nobody wants to be left out of a joke.**

Since many of you have forgotten what it is like to be a student, think of the last time that you were in church. (For some of you it was less than a week ago and for others, years.) At some point in one or more of the meetings, most likely you were not paying attention to the speaker or the teacher. He or she was telling you how your soul could be saved or how to gain an eternal existence of joy, or something else important, meaningful, and spiritually uplifting. Maybe the minister was even supplying instruction as to how to avoid burning for all time in inextinguishable fire and brimstone. Did you listen? Did you care? Huh, did ya? But, when members of the congregation began to laugh, what did you do? I'll tell you what you did. You said, "Huh? What? What was that? What did he (she) say? C'mon tell me what was so funny."

We may not care about our eternal existence, but we've got to know what was so funny. From that point on, we begin paying closer attention to the message, just in case something else funny is shared. How interesting it is to note that, along the way, we learn stuff! Nobody wants to be left out of a joke. In fact, I've noticed that people readily admit to lying, cheating, stealing, Botox injections, hair plugs, and all manner of lawlessness—but almost no one will admit to lacking a sense of humor.

> I've noticed that people readily admit to lying, cheating, stealing, Botox injections, hair plugs, and all manner of lawlessness—but almost no one will admit to lacking a sense of humor.

Now, if we as adults enjoy an occasional bit of humor to help capture and keep our attention, then why aren't we doing a better job of sharing humor with our students? A little bit of humor goes a long way in grabbing and maintaining students' attention.

On several occasions when I have been giving a presentation, some educator has cornered me to say, "I don't think that I should have to be an entertainer for my students. They should just come to my class wanting to learn. Why should I have to be funny while teaching my material?"

In response I say, "Security, please escort that person out of here!" Then I continue, "You can do whatever you want. You certainly do have a choice. You can battle for your students' attention your entire teaching life. Or, you can be creative and have some fun along the way while you gain and retain their attention."

## Humor Promotes Health

Have you ever laughed so hard that your sides hurt? Wouldn't you rather laugh a lot than do a thousand sit-ups? Actually, to achieve the greatest health benefit, you should do sit-ups while listening to a good comedy routine. The point is: laugh a lot and have tight abs; laugh and do sit-ups and have even tighter abs; laugh, do sit-ups, and take steroids and you'll have great big tight abs with a million zits (and when you're not laughing . . . . . . . scream a lot). *Note to reader: The publisher and author of this book in no way advocate the use of steroids for teachers. This is a joke—not the part about laughter functioning like exercise for your body, though—just the steroid part.*

> **Laughter (in the right amounts) can actually amount to an aerobic workout.**

Researchers claim that laughter (in the right amounts) can actually amount to an aerobic workout. (The details and references to the previous statement will be included in the boring section at the end of this chapter.) Laughter helps pump carbon dioxide out of the lungs and feeds oxygen to the brain. Have you ever laughed until you cried? Laughing yourself to tears actually helps cleanse your eyes and tear ducts. Experiencing humorous situations or finding humor in difficult situations causes the muscles to relax and increases the flow of adrenaline. The more you laugh, the more your cardiovascular system exercises. Everyone should set aside time every day to laugh and enjoy a healthier lifestyle.

The body is smart. All kinds of interesting chemical things happen in your body when you laugh. You actually **do** begin to feel better—physiologically. It's almost as if you can trick yourself into feeling better by laughing; but it's no trick. It's the way the body is designed. You don't even have to experience anything humorous; just start laughing. Try it. The next time you're frustrated while standing in a quarter-mile-long line at Wal-Mart, just start laughing. You'll feel better and you'll find yourself at the front of the line much quicker, too.

*"Stop! You're killing me!"*

You can also try this in your principal's office the next time you're in trouble for taking your students outside to play a learning game that was not approved in octuplicate (a real word) forms by the principal, district superintendent, local school board, state superintendent, federal NCLB committee, Homeland Security, World Allergy Organization, and the Boy Scouts and Girl Scouts of America. Just start laughing hysterically and walk out. I did it to four different principals in one year. It felt wonderful. (I'll let you draw your own conclusions as to why I had four different principals in one year.) Try it. You'll feel great—at least until you come back the next day and find somebody else teaching your classes. *Note to reader: Do not attempt laughing hysterically at your principal while he or she is disciplining you—until you have tenure. Then laugh your head off whenever you want.*

## Humor Relieves Pain

Humor has also been considered an analgesic. Norman Cousins claims to have cured himself from a painful collagen disease that gave him a 1-in-500 chance of survival. He insists that humor gave him the will to live and the ability to withstand the excruciating physical pain. Any time the pain

seemed unbearable, he read humorous books or watched funny videos to get relief. Numerous other patients and medical personnel have noted that a sense of humor goes a long way toward helping people cope with or recover from difficult medical problems, or even beat the odds of survival.

Check your students' faces every once in a while. Don't they appear to be in some pain as they sort through difficult literary works; compute complicated math problems; conjugate foreign language verbs; or listen to a dull, non-interactive, irrelevant, recycled history lecture? Teachers can help alleviate that pain by sharing or encouraging humor in their classrooms. A teacher often feels grief and pain, as well, while the students are tortured with relentless boredom and repetition. Appease your own pain (and theirs) with some humor during those times. As long as they know your expectations, the students will quickly get right back to work. *Note to reader: Laughter may not be an analgesic soon after a C-section or for those suffering from a hernia.*

## Humor Helps the Brain Learn

The world of neuroscience has handed educators some marvelous understandings about how the brain learns. From this we know that humor actually enables the brain to do its job better. We have learned that strong emotions help the brain attend to ideas, find meaning, and retain concepts. And humor is a tool that releases emotions such as joy, or even loss, sadness, or embarrassment. Furthermore, we now know that human brains are social. They learn (and remember what they learn) best in communication with others. This knowledge sets a strong case for collaborative classroom experiences. It also makes a strong case for humor—a social activity that eases many otherwise scary or tense group-learning situations.

## Humor Shapes Examples That Students Remember

Studies of students at all levels (discussed in the extremely boring section at the end of this chapter) show that they remember a significantly greater amount of material when it is presented in a humorous fashion. As a lead-in to a chapter on body parts in my Spanish classes, I tell my students a short story about my early days in Chile. I first explain the difference between manos (hands) and monos (monkeys). Then I describe how I told a group of runners in Chile that it is best to put your monkeys on your head in order to expand your lungs and take in more oxygen. That's not a tremendously funny story, but it is to a group of students trying to learn a list of vocabulary words. They love to know that their teacher makes mistakes and has looked foolish with the subject that he or she now teaches. It gives them more confidence and enjoyment in a subject area that may be hard for them.

**Humor actually enables the brain to do its job better.**

I go on to describe and demonstrate to my students what those young runners' faces looked like after I told them to put some monkeys on their heads. Then I get a little sarcastic with my own stupidity. "What's the matter? Haven't you ever seen monkeys help someone breathe? They sit on your head and scoop up lots of air and then slam it in your nose and mouth. Come on, you'll love it. Now, everybody put as many monkeys as you can on your head."

After a little session like that, the students giggle their way through the rest of the vocabulary list, picturing what their teacher must have looked like in that situation. In that particular chapter we also sing "Cabeza, hombros, rodillas, pies" (Head, shoulders, knees, and toes). They animate it while singing, laughing all the while, and yet they learn all of the words and how to use them appropriately. You don't have to have a story or a song for every word or every assignment. Just do it often enough to keep their attention.

## Humor Fights Stress

Humor helps release some of the stress that can build up for students in countless situations—stress that affects school attitudes, relationships, and performances. It can do the same for administrators and teachers. Humor reduces stress, improves communication in schools, and increases productivity. In times of stress, humor can neutralize the emotionally-charged atmosphere. In contrast, a teacher or administrator who does not share a sense of humor may become a source of much stress to their students or other staff members. In fact, teachers often identify their principals as causing stress or causing stressful situations for them. And students often feel the same about their teachers.

Our students face one stressful situation after another—all day—every day. Here are just a few examples: pop quizzes, exams, standardized tests, homework, mean teachers, crabby parents, psycho coaches, cranky librarians, zit outbreaks, bullies on the playground and in the halls, riding the bus with 59 other kids (some sickening, some annoying, some downright terrifying), wondering if a parent or assigned guardian will remember to pick up them up after school, boyfriend or girlfriend problems or lack of a boyfriend or girlfriend, gas, being called on while not paying attention in class, deciding whether it's better to act like you're paying attention when you're really not or to act like you're not paying attention when you really are, remembering what time to call or text friends, remembering what time the secret meeting in the bathroom was scheduled, and another round of life success-or-failure-determining standardized tests—all while trying to look good and act cool.

## Humor Eases Tension

This section may seem a little bit like the stress section, except—well, it just is. However, this has more to do with conditions that have built into a tightly-stretched, ready-to-snap atmosphere between individuals or groups, as opposed to stress, which is often held inside the individual. Humor eases social conflicts and irritations. Since the days of the court jesters, it has been used to reduce tension.

Here's an example of a risk I took to relieve some major-league tension during my stint as a high school teacher. One afternoon in early spring, many of the school's students were involved in a large brawl across the street from campus. The next day, the tension was palpable. Another fight seemed inevitable. Students were taking sides, arguing the different issues, and making claims about which side would win the fight next time (and why and how).

After overhearing plans for a much larger fight with intent to do even more damage to individuals and property, I tried to hold a serious discussion with my students about the possible ramifications of such an altercation. They seemed to pay attention and their faces looked pensive. But I noticed no change of heart, and none of the students would talk to me about it. Thus I took it upon myself to make an announcement. I knew that the principal would never approve it, so I didn't ask. I got on the microphone thingy and announced the following to the entire student body: "The administration has asked that those participating in tomorrow's rumble please limit your weapons to non-perishable food items, so that afterwards they can be donated to the homeless and the needy."

> Our students face one stressful situation after another—all day—every day.

No fight took place. I can't say for sure that the joke saved the day (even though I am sure it did), but many teachers told me how funny it was and that their students all started laughing and talking about how silly that would be—fighting with food items. I had to have a "special meeting" with the principal, but there wasn't a fight, tension eased within the student body, and I got to keep my job (after I apologized to the principal on bended knee and with bowed head).

## Humor Promotes Creativity

The presence of laughter tends to open a learner's mind to divergent thinking that has been previously suppressed by the critical, traditional self. In an environment of fun and creativity, new, sometimes unlikely and outrageous ideas often surface. As the fun increases, so does the level of student participation. In order to understand, interpret, or "get" many jokes, a person must think in an uncommon way. Students have to adjust perspective to figure out the humor or to create their own jokes. By using more humor in school, we lay the groundwork for expanding creativity. Jokes, puns, quips,

> **More creative ideas are generated in humorous environments than in non-humorous environments.**

extraordinary twists on ordinary things—these all help students push the boundaries of thinking skills. Problem-solving abilities increase, because students practice the art of examining a situation from different perspectives.

A sense of humor is often associated with creativity. More creative ideas are generated in humorous environments than in non-humorous environments. Both humor and creativity involve working with (oops, I should say **playing** with) ideas. As students communicate, participate, and interact more (all outcomes of humorous situations), their inhibitions are lowered, and they produce more creative ideas. Sharing humor also incurs a certain level of risk. People may not laugh. What a terrible thought! Producing creative, original ideas thus necessitates risk taking—another strategy that fosters creativity.

Southwest Airlines, which is one of the few airlines consistently turning a profit at the time this book was written, often seeks creative ideas from its employees. The company encourages fun on the job, because the executives know that fun produces more creative solutions to problems—which eventually increase profits. In fact, Southwest Airlines estimates that its employees' creative ideas have saved the company millions of dollars each year. Are your students prepared to work for a company like that? Or when asked a question by their employer, will they answer with, "What are my options?"

## Boring Research Section (Well, sort of, maybe)

Okay, now for the boring research-type stuff. Just skip to the next chapter if you want. But remember, you can't say you read the book if you didn't read the entire book. Sorry, I don't make the rules. You'll have to say, "I read parts of the book." You choose. I'll try to make this section kind of short and not too way completely boring, dude.

*Note to reader: Okay, I'll let you in on a secret, but don't you dare tell anyone else I said this: It is cool to say that research is boring. To keep my cool-guy reputation, I'm making that my official line. But actually, it is kind of amazing to read about the measurable stuff that verifies humor's benefits. I might even go so far as to say it is way cool to learn that science tells us what good teachers have instinctively known for centuries about humor.*

Author G. A. Fine (1983) found that, since members of groups share experiences in common, any group member can refer to these experiences with an expectation that she or he will be understood by other members of the group. Humor is particularly useful for this, in that it allows the group to refer to a wide range of content that could not be expressed otherwise. One of the main goals of any group should be to remain unified in the midst of actual or potential forces that might upset or threaten it. A class that is unified by pleasant experiences (such as laughter and humor) has a better chance of weathering disagreements, disruptions, and difficulties than a class without those humorous bonding experiences. Schools and their cultures can benefit from a well-developed sense of humor, as they are often threatened with change, budget difficulties, equipment shortages, community scrutiny, and a host of other scary forces.

Psychiatrist Viktor Frankl (1963) shows the power that humor can have on the climate of an organization. Frankl encourages his clients to exaggerate their symptoms to the point of absurdity, which enables them to laugh at their own problems. He first learned of this technique when he was a prisoner in a concentration camp in World War II Germany. The strategy helped him and his friends to noticeably change the climate of the camp in a positive manner. He even attributes humor to giving them hope and making the unbearable seem capable of being borne.

Although the term "stress" is used liberally in today's society, it is not likely that any two individuals claiming to be stressed will be experiencing the same feelings (Edworthy, 2000). When a person is exposed to a stressor, a number of changes may be observed—including psychological, physiological, and overt behavioral changes. With respect to psychological events, one may observe anxiety, feelings of distress, and evidence of a strong tendency to avoid the situation. With respect to physiological events, one may observe changes in heart rate and blood pressure. And with respect to the overt behavioral responses, one may observe trembling, stuttering, and physical avoidance of the stressor (Riley & Furedy, 1985).

The results of a study by Adair and Siegel (1984) indicate that humor improves the level of performance during a stressful task. After a pretest administration of the dependent measure, 40 college students performed a mathematics test under one of four experimental conditions: high stress, moderate stress, presence of humor, or absence of humor. Analyses of the results showed that the presence of humor in moderate and high stress conditions improved the level of task performance. Humor not only relieves stress in the workplace, but can also be used to improve worker performance (Malone, 1980).

> Researchers conclude that humor increases self-esteem in students.

In order to better understand the effects of humor on stress, Berk, Tan, Fry, Napier, Lee, Hubbard, Lewis, and Eby (1989) performed a study of the effects of laughter on certain stress hormones. The authors studied 10 healthy male subjects not taking supplemental drugs or medication. There were five experimental subjects and five control subjects. A skilled physician was assigned to each subject to obtain blood samples in a relaxed manner. The subjects rested for 15 minutes after IV placement. Blood samples were taken every 10 minutes. The five experimental subjects viewed a 60-minute humor video and the five control subjects did not. Three blood samples were taken before laughter intervention, six during laughter intervention, and three after laughter intervention. Samples for the control group were taken at equal intervals, but no laughter intervention was used. The data showed that laughter significantly decreased stress hormones. The authors feel that these results imply that laughter causes a reversal of stress hormones, therefore relieving stress on the body and mind.

Fry and Salameh (1987) show that laughing 100 times a day is the cardiovascular equivalent of 10 minutes of a strenuous exercise like rowing or jogging. *Note to reader: Don't combine the two. I tried jogging in a rowboat one time in hopes of doubling my workout potential—not a good idea.* Fry and Salameh have also determined that the body releases its own natural painkillers (endorphins) when laughter occurs—thereby reducing stress. According to Chapman and Foot (1996), all researchers who have examined the effects of humor on stress agree that possessing and using a sense of humor is healthy and desirable.

Humor releases some of the tension that otherwise might exist between the principal, teachers, and students. The use of humor improves morale, reduces stress, and improves communication in schools—all of which improve productivity. In times of stress, tragedy, and crisis, humor is a technique used for neutralizing the emotionally-charged area. For the moment that humor is used, the burden is forgotten (Moody, 1978).

In a self-esteem study by LaFave, Haddad, and Maesen (1996), college students were subjected to a series of 20 jokes. Afterwards, students were shown to have an increase in reinforcement happiness, which the authors interpret as higher self-esteem. Therefore, they conclude that humor increases self-esteem in students. Informal observations by Chapman (1983) at several elementary schools revealed that even elementary school children use humor to raise self-esteem.

Ellet and Walberg (1979) suggest that the behavior of a principal in school has a major influence on the attitudes and behaviors of teachers. In turn, they say the attitudes and behaviors of teachers will affect student development. Teachers who are dissatisfied with work not only find themselves suffering, but their students suffer also (Csikszentmihalyi & McCormack, 1986; Firestone & Rosenblum, 1988; Rosenholtz, 1989). However, when teachers are more satisfied with their jobs, they are more effective in the classroom (Anderman, Belzer, & Smith, 1991). And to tie this paragraph together, Hurren (me) (2006) found that when principals share more humor in school, their teachers are more satisfied with their jobs, and therefore, more effective in the classroom. How cool is that? I've always wanted to cite my own research. Now, I've done it. Time to set a new goal.

Wilson and Cameron (1994) studied, coded, and analyzed 28 student teachers' journal entries during a three-week practicum experience. They found that teachers who use and encourage laughter in the classroom have students who learn quickly, retain more, and have fewer classroom problems. According to the authors, this is due to the humor causing a more relaxed, healthy work environment that stimulates more productivity.

Chapman and Crompton (1978) used five- and six-year-old boys and girls to test the effects of humor on recall. The children were randomly assigned to one of two groups. Each group saw a series of 10 slides—each one of a different animal. Every slide was accompanied by a simple statement about spelling. For example, when a tiger was shown, "t is for tiger," accompanied the picture. One group of 15 saw slides of animals that had previously been determined as humorous by children of the same age. The other group of 15 saw slides that had been determined as non-humorous. A recall quiz immediately followed the presentation of the slides. The humorous slides facilitated better recall with a mean score of 5.3 compared to 3.4 for the non-humorous slides. This was shown to be significant at the $p < .05$ level.

Ziv (1976) used a sample of 282 high school students to test the influence of humor on creativity. The students were divided into four groups. All groups were given Form A of a verbal creativity test. Three weeks later, groups one and three were given Form B of the verbal creativity test after listening to a humorous record. Groups two and four were given the same task, without having listened to the record. An analysis of variance was performed on the test scores. No significant difference was found on pretest scores, but there was a significant difference found on posttest scores. Significance was found at the $p < .001$ level between the scores of treatment groups versus non-treatment groups. The results of this study show that humorous stimuli increase creative

> Brains learn best in concert with other brains. Humor is a great tool to build social interaction and collaboration.

thinking in high school students. These results justify Goodman's (1983) theory that humor serves to capture students' attention, hold their attention, and free them from distractions, so that they can and do perform more creative work of a higher quality.

Researchers Renate and Geoffrey Caine have articulated twelve brain-mind principles of brain-compatible learning. These principles are derived from understandings about the structure of the brain and how it works. One of the principles is this: the search for meaning comes through patterning. Another brain-mind principle is this: Emotions are critical to patterning. Students learn, understand, and remember better those ideas that are connected to or arouse strong emotions. Humor releases emotion, and thus is a recommended classroom strategy by those who apply brain research to educational settings. Another of the twelve principles is this: The brain is social. Brains learn best in concert with other brains. Again, humor is a great tool to build social interaction and collaboration (Caine and Caine, 1991).

Three basic strategies for the learning environment follow from the principles of brain-based learning. One of them is that the brain learns best in a setting and state of relaxed (and safe) alertness (Caine, Caine, McClintic, and Klimek, 2004). Teachers must eliminate fear for learners while maintaining a highly challenging environment. Humor is uniquely fitting for this purpose. It cuts through fear while keeping the brain alert to "get" the joke.

There, that wasn't too terrible. Was it? Don't answer that.

*"Before I get to the really funny stuff, I'd like to take twenty minutes to share the research I put into making this hilarious routine."*

## Chapter Summary

- There are a lot of benefits to using humor in school.

- These benefits are discussed herein.

- These benefits are supported by research.

- Research is boring (mostly).

## Summary of the Summary

Humor is good; research is boring.

# 4

## Dump the Golden Rule of Classroom Management

### Starting the Year

*"Your honor, I will prove that the defendant blatantly smiled twice in front of her Algebra class on May 5."*

"Don't let your students see you smile until December." That is the adage—even the golden rule that all too many teachers practice, and by the time December actually rolls around, those same teachers' faces are frozen (or rusted) into cranky, nasty, mean-looking ogre masks. Then they find it impossible to smile or enjoy their students without a good thawing or 2½ cans of WD40. Or, they have simply forgotten how to smile or have fun at all. If this is your motto and you're in the former category (frozen or rusted face), you can wait for further global warming or for Dorothy and the Tin Man to come rescue you. If you're in the latter category (forgotten how to smile), I can help.

## Whose Idea Was This, Anyway?

"Don't let your students see you smile until December."
Why? I've always wondered about that. College professors in education departments warn their students, "Don't let your students see you smile until December." School administrators warn their teachers at the start of each year. "Don't let your students see you smile until December." Mentors with craggy faces warn the new teachers, "Don't let your students see you smile until December." By the time a new teacher sets up his first classroom, he has been warned over 543 times by more than 22 people, "Don't let your students see you smile until December." One of my reasons for writing, "Don't let your students see you smile until December," "Don't let your students see you smile until December," "Don't let your students see you smile until December," "Don't let your students see you smile until December" so many times is that I want you to be sick of seeing, hearing, and thinking, "Don't let your students see you smile until December." If you ever see it or hear it again, you should feel an immediate desire to wretch. But hopefully you will control this heaving impulse for the moment and simply ask, "Why?" Or ask, "Why not?" Whatever question you ask, you will probably get one of the following answers:

1. "You don't know why?"

2. "Why??? Are you really asking me why?"

3. "Because, ummmmm. What kind of a question is that?"

4. "Do you really need to ask that question?"

5. "Haven't you ever been around students this age before?"

6. "What are they teaching you at that university?"

7. "Welllllllll, everybody knows why."

When people give me answer number 7, I ask another question, "Do you?" That causes them to actually have to think a little bit, so they squint their eyes and wrinkle an already wrinklefied forehead as if they've just sat on a tack that was strategically placed on their chair, and then they say one of the following:

1. "You don't know why?"

2. "Why??? Are you really asking me why?"

3. "Because, ummmmm. What kind of a question is that?"

4. "Do you really need to ask that question?"

5. "Haven't you ever been around students this age before?"

6. "What are they teaching you at that university?"

At this point I usually want to say, "It's no fair answering my question with a question that doesn't answer the question that I first questioned." But for your benefit, I've compiled the following list of answers to the above-mentioned, corresponding six questions. Take care to memorize which answers correspond to which questions.

1. "No."

2. "Yes."

3. "Rhetorical. Or maybe it's a divergent, high-order thinking, cognitive question that requires analysis, synthesis, and evaluation."

4. "Yes. No. Maybe. I don't know."

5. "Yes, I was a student this age—twice, thanks to teachers like you."

6. "They are teaching me to supply hands-on learning experiences of exploration and discovery, facilitate long-lasting and meaningful learning, connect instruction to students' real-life experiences, maintain a positive classroom atmosphere, assess effectively and fairly, and to have fun with my students."

## Escape from the Trap

I'm embarrassed to admit that I almost fell for the trap that was set for me my first year of teaching. A few college professors had said, "Don't let your students see you smile until December." (Wretch) My principal reminded me as he gave me my first set of school keys, "Now remember, don't let your students see you smile until December." (Spew) The experienced but cranky teacher across the hall stopped in my doorway the first day of classes and said, "Hey, I guess you're new here. Let me just say that as far as these students are concerned, don't let them see you smile until December." (Yack)

So, I started my first day of teaching middle school with a prepared speech about rules, hard work, school is not supposed to be fun, obey or go to the office, tough discipline, and so on and so on. For about four or five minutes, I held firm with a strong voice and a pre-crotchety face. My students were staring at me, some in fear. Others had that look on their faces that told me they were saying to themselves, "Dude, zip it. You're boring us to death—just like all the other teachers."

*I started to listen to myself. I **was** boring. Worse than that, I sounded scary, aggressive, and hostile.*

Then, I started to listen to myself. I **was** boring. Worse than that, I sounded scary,

*Humor in School is Serious Business*

aggressive, and hostile. Suddenly, I started laughing. I laughed so hard that I had to bend over to catch my breath.

Ask students, "What do you want to do this year and how are we going to maintain order so that we can do it?"

When I looked up, there were fifty-seven eyes looking at me in terror. (One boy wore an eye patch.) No teacher had ever laughed in front of them before, and it scared them. That's when I first realized that laughing might be more effective at capturing and holding their attention than getting mad and yelling. After I caught my breath and let out a long sigh, a student dared ask, "What's wrong with you?"

I answered, "I just heard my own voice trying to be mean and tough. That's not who I am. Forget everything I just said. Now, what do you want to do this year and how are we going to maintain order so that we can do it?"

I hurriedly grabbed a piece of chalk, thinking that their answers would be flying at me a mile-a-minute. I held my hand high on the chalkboard, ready to write a long list of suggestions. Silence (except for a cricket chirping in the back left corner). As my arm began to tire, grow heavy, and then cramp, I decided to shove my students. I mean, I pushed them for answers. "Come on. There must be something that you are hoping, wishing, and dreaming about doing in this class."

"Sleep," someone whispered to a few giggles from classmates. I wrote "sleep" on the board. Students looked at each other with disbelief in their eyes—partly from the realization that I had heard the whispered comment from the back of the room, partly because I didn't get mad, and partly because I wrote the comment on the board.

*Humor in School is Serious Business*

"Watch movies," another student half uttered, half mumbled.

I wrote "movies" on the board. There were more doubtful looks, but students started to sit up and take notice.

"Eat in class," somebody said with a little more gusto in his voice.

"Food," went on the board.

"Play games," a girl hollered.

And so it went, with suggestions to chew gum, play, go outside, play outside, have free days, write notes to each other, play music, and go on field trips. About the time that I was thinking, "What was I thinking?" somebody said, "When I go to a Mexican restaurant, I want to be able to understand what all of the workers are saying and order in Spanish like I know what I'm doing."

I dropped the chalk on the floor and clutched my chest. After a few moments, I started hitting the left side of my chest with my right fist, as if trying to get my heart started beating again. "Now why on earth would you want to do that?" I gasped.

"Because I'm tired of feeling stupid in Mexican restaurants, and I love the food."

"Anybody else tired of feeling stupid when people speak Spanish around you?" About half of the students raised their hands to half-mast. "So what do you want to do about it?"

"I guess, learn Spanish," a boy in the middle of the room said with a sad look on his face.

"YES!!!" I screamed at the top of my lungs, and I ran over

*Humor in School is Serious Business*

to give him a high-five—knocking over an empty desk in the process.

"I want to be able to read the Spanish newspaper that's given away in a lot of the stores."

"I want to know what people are saying about me in grocery store lines."

"I want to understand what little Spanish-speaking children are saying on the bus."

"I want to understand the Spanish TV channels, especially the commercials."

*This is one of the first things that all teachers must do every school year: help students take ownership of their own learning.*

The ideas were coming so fast that I couldn't keep pace with the students. I was just scribbling on the chalkboard. Then a student in the left, center-back, middle-edge, corner-side of the classroom said, "I just want to be able to speak Spanish and sound like I know Spanish."

So this is one of the first things that all teachers must do every school year: help students take ownership of their own learning. They will offer fun, creative, and exciting ideas to enhance their learning experiences and make the classroom a more enjoyable place to be. The classroom experiences are then more meaningful to the students, and their learning is real, relevant, and long lasting.

When we had filled two chalkboards full of ideas, I told the students there would be a few items that I would cross off the list because of laws or schoolwide rules; but the only three that I really had to cross off were "sleeping," "free days," and "chewing gum." Chewing gum may have its place in other classes, but in a Spanish class, rolling the double "r" with gum in the mouth will most likely result in an innocent victim making an unexpected trip to the barber. Everything else they suggested could easily be done within a learning context. It is not too hard to adjust lesson plans to include students' good ideas and give them a sense of ownership of the learning process. Remember, I'm not suggesting that you eliminate material. I'm suggesting that you add students' motivational ideas to your methods of instruction. How to use most of the aforementioned ideas will be discussed more completely in future chapters.

Something else happened besides gathering a list of goals and ideas for the year. We had fun. The beginning-of-the-year anxiety and discomfort disappeared. Students relaxed with the new teacher and with each other. We began to build camaraderie. We started the school year feeling good about each other—all because the teacher traded in the "Don't smile" rule for some down-to-earth humor.

## Ask the Students, Already

The next step is to ask the students how we are going to accomplish all of these ideas and how we are going to maintain order while learning. I won't go into great detail here, because it's not really that comical, but it is fun for students to offer their own classroom procedures and consequences. They are almost always more strict than I would be. (They don't know that.) I generally have to toss out some of their ideas that constitute unusually cruel punishment. For example: sit against the wall with your thighs parallel to the floor for five minutes, or do 50 push-ups or 100 sit-ups, or go the office.

Sending a student to the office, by the way, is generally a complete waste of time. It wastes the administrator's time by having him or her take care of a problem that you most likely could have and should have resolved. It wastes your (the teacher's) time, because when the student comes back to your class you are going to have to help him or her catch up to the rest of the students, and by this time, the student dislikes you and your class and the material. So you have to work harder to get this student to pay attention and learn. It also wastes the student's time by being out of class and doing absolutely nothing productive. (Generally she or he sits in a chair waiting to see an administrator while making faces at other students who are wandering the halls, going to the restroom, delivering messages to the office, or simply lost and can't find their way home.) These students even communicate with each other through secretive hand maneuvers and unbreakable codes of facial gestures.

*"The kid sitting behind me in Spanish class tried to roll his 'r's' with bubblegum in his mouth."*

After 17 years of research, fieldwork, documentation, observations, coding, decoding, recoding, statistical analysis, data analysis, triangulation, and silent interviews, I believe that I have broken the code: When one student squints the eyes, purses the lips in a downward fashion, and shows the inside (palms) of both hands about waist high, it means, "Yo, tsst, pbbt?" And when a student rolls the eyes high and to the right with a slight jerk of the head in the same direction while puckering the lips tightly and raising the shoulders a half inch, it means, "Mr. Krankity's all whackity whack!" Now,

I have no idea what any of that means, but if you would like to perform a collaborative follow-up study on modern student translations, feel free to e-mail me at *blhurren@una.edu* when you are finished with the study.

Anyway, back to my earlier point: You and your students can generate several long lists of procedures and consequences for your class and then vote on those that are feasible and legal. Usually my students decide that disruptions like excessive talking in English (not a good idea when you're trying to learn Spanish), pestering other students, throwing small objects, littering, chewing gum, or playing paper football result in the guilty student(s) apologizing to the class and staying after class to help clean up the room and rearrange the desks. Only major offenses such as fighting, anything of a sexual nature, or possession of drugs would result in a visit to the administration. Throwing desks, chairs, fellow students, or the teacher would result in a measurement for distance and a possible record, followed by a parent conference.

After we have decided upon 10 to 12 procedures or rules and 3 to 5 consequences, we have a serious talk about complying with the procedures so that we can realize all of the fun things that we hope to accomplish—while learning! If someone doesn't comply, we will stick to the consequences. I remind students that we will have a lot of fun in my class, but that is not an excuse or reason to behave inappropriately.

This next step may seem obvious, but new teachers may need to be reminded of it. Tell your students (in your rarely used serious voice) that certain behaviors (alcohol and drug use or possession, weapons, certain language, and any abusive actions or disrespect to other persons) will not be tolerated.

Type your procedures and consequences and give each student two copies. Have them and a parent or guardian sign one copy and a statement that they "agree to have fun in class, but will follow agreed-upon procedures and consequences." Add your own humorous procedures to those already listed. A few examples are found below. Check for more ideas in Chapter 7. Yes, it is possible to insert humor into even such serious business as rules and procedures.

## CLASSROOM PROCEDURES

- No cell phones, pagers, beepers, CD players, or MP3 players allowed in class. Also not allowed: transistor radios, 8-track tape players, record players, rotary telephones, tanning beds, big-screen TVs, boomboxes, phonographs, hi-fi stereos, or 35 mm projectors.

- During class, please turn off all motorized vehicles, including: cars, pick-up trucks, vans, SUVs, go-carts, minibikes, motorcycles, 18-wheelers, dump trucks, and front-end loaders.

- No whining in class; however, soft whimpering is allowed upon preapproval from the teacher.

# Nine Alternatives to the "Don't Smile" Rule

As a student and as a teacher, I have often thought about how difficult it is to end summer break and begin school again. The first days and weeks of school, though exciting, are stressful for teachers and students. Therefore, we teachers should do whatever we can to alleviate some of that pain and suffering and set a positive climate for the year of living and learning together that lies ahead. There are possibilities for things to do that follow a different course than the "Don't smile" philosophy. Here are some of the things that I have used with my students. Try them, or use them to spark your own ideas or your own version of these ideas. Be sure that whatever you do to start the year off right is fitting with your personality and the needs of your students. Make sure **you** participate in any activities you design to start the school year right. Students love to find out about their teachers' lives and interests. Even more important, your participation in the activities and games gives students the important message that you are all in this together.

## 1. Hey, Get to Know Me!

I like to start the first day of class with a "Get-to-know-me" activity that I adapted (stole) from John Lovitz, comedian. Most middle school and high school students dislike (or at least pretend that or think that they are supposed to hate the guts of) their teachers from the very start of the school year, so I just tell my students that I know that. "Now, I know that you hate me and my class, and this prison of a school, and Mrs. Ann Gree the principal, and Sir Lee the vice principal, and Ms. Druly the lunch lady, and Mr. Ira Tabul the custodian, and Miss Era T. Bulle the librarian, and even Mrs. Rue Moore the office secretary. But I want you all to know that not all of us are crummy, hateful, evil people. Let me read a few letters that I have received over the years from former students who were just like you at one time in their lives."

I then pull out a few envelopes with stamps and addresses on them and remove the letters and begin reading.

> Dear Mr. Hurren,
> I want to thank you for helping me
> so much in your class. Before I took your class, I was
> nobody, a nothing, a zero, a loser, and nobody knew
> that I even existed. I used to have the voice of a
> little girl. Then I took your class."

At this point I start to raise my voice, getting louder as I progress.

> "Now, my friends know me as Bruce Springsteen."

Then I shout, "GET TO KNOW ME!"

I immediately follow that letter with another. They don't realize right away that I am just getting their attention. Some of them even glance at each other with incredulous looks of "Hmm, wow. Really?" Others seem to be wondering who in the world Bruce Springsteen is. Then I read the next letter:

> "Dear Mr. Hurren, I want to thank you for helping me so much in your class. Before I took your class, I was a nobody, a nothing, a zero, a loser and nobody knew that I even existed. I had a weak backhand and no top spin. Then I took your class. Now my friends know me as Maria Sharapova. GET TO KNOW ME!"

Now the students look confused. It's time to read the next letter:

*"Dear Mr. Hurren, I want to thank you for helping me so much in your class. Before I took your class, I was a nobody, a nothing, a zero, a loser, and nobody knew that I even existed. I was scared to try out for sports teams. Then I took your class. Now my friends know me as Peyton Manning. GET TO KNOW ME!"*

Use any celebrity, teacher, or administrator that you want. You can even use accents to add authenticity to the presentation of a letter. I know that it sounds goofy, but students love to hear teachers use fake accents. Take a little time to practice your accents and facial expressions in front of the mirror and you will be more comfortable with it. Two of the keys to pulling off the "Get to know me" activity are to shout at the right time and keep a straight face. Again, practice helps.

*"Here's getting to know me, kids."*

*Note to reader: Eventually, your friends, spouse, and other family members get used to your practicing accents and faces . . . sort of. After 20 years, my wife still isn't used to me calling her "Yo Adrian," but that's her problem. Nevertheless, she did say that I look much better when I twist my lips crooked, talk out of the side of my mouth, droop one eye half closed, and drool on myself.*

*There is nothing more important you can do in the first days of school than to show students that you are interested in their dreams, wishes, and preferences.*

## 2. What About You?

On one of the first days in the school year, pass out an index card to each student. Each student writes his or her name, class period, favorite book, the last book that was read voluntarily (with the year it was read), and favorite dessert topping. Obviously, you can create your own list of things to ask, substituting things such as favorite pizza topping, condiment, dessert, dream, board game, free-time activity, etc. Ask students to also write one or two lines about something funny, interesting, or different that has happened to them in their lives.

Collect these cards and ask students to share their funny, interesting, or different stories with the whole class. This accomplishes a few things all at once: It gets your class off to a fun start, helps students relax and begin to enjoy class, peaks students' curiosity about what this class will be like, lets students know a bit about each other and begin to learn names, and helps me get to know my students (as well as remember their names). I'm not a natural at remembering names, but if I have my index cards with something funny or interesting about each student, then I can practice and remember their names much faster. The stuff on these cards associates the names with something personal. There is nothing more important you can do in the first days of school than to show students that you are interested in their dreams, wishes, and preferences.

### 3. Letters to Former Teachers

Give students a few minutes to think about teachers that have had a positive impact on their lives or learning. I have found that many students often say they don't care for their current teachers, but generally have fond memories of former teachers. Ask them to choose one and write a letter to that teacher. Encourage them to include specific details of how that teacher helped them learn. Then find time for students to talk about these teachers. This can set a hopeful and positive atmosphere as they recall and recount exciting and fun learning activities from past school days. You can then read the letters before delivering them to the teachers, in order to find out about your students' likes, dislikes, personalities, and writing styles. You might also be inspired to modify and use some of the activities described in the letters. (Share letters with their "recipients" only with permission from students.)

### 4. Welcome to Zippity-Do Airlines

Give your first day opening welcome and instructions as if you were an airline pilot. It is even more effective if you borrow a microphone and speaker from your library and cup your hands over your mouth and the microphone as you speak. "Krrjjcck, ahhh, this is your captain speaking. Krrjjcck, ahhh, I'd like to welcome each and every one of you to my fun and exciting flight to Mathzania (Historylandia, Englishtonia, Biologyria, Grade Threetown, Kindergartenville)," and so on.

"This will be one of the most exhilarating, memorable learning trips that you have ever taken. Krrjjcck, ahhh, however, in order to enjoy this trip to its fullest, we must follow certain guidelines. Throughout this flight you will be expected to . . ." (and then you can launch into some of your expectations). I like to periodically motion to the door and aisles as the flight attendants do, just for fun.

I end by saying, "So if you will now fasten your seatbelts, we'll put this classroom in motion." This activity actually led to my students calling me *El Capitán* as my name/title in Spanish classes.

## 5. Name Games

Name games always help students and teachers get to know each other. Many versions exist; simply choose one that seems to fit your particular age group and your personality—and try to add some humor to whatever game you use. You can have each student introduce herself or himself and name an animal that rhymes with or starts with the same letter as her or his name. For example: "My name is Jason the Jaguar" or "My name is Amanda the Panda." (Have them make a connection between their name and the animal that will help everyone remember the name, as well as learn something about them.) You can do the same thing with likes and dislikes. For example: "My name is Steve and I like steak and stir-fry, but I don't like stinky stuff." Get creative and have your students use favorite snack foods, condiments, ice-cream flavors, pizza toppings, colors, activities, behaviors, words, or anything else (appropriate) that you concoct.

Students can invent new All-Star Wrestling (or other sport) names. For example: "My name is Krazy Kikkin Kim" or "My name is Benjamin the Bonecrusher." Give a few guidelines and examples to make sure that everybody can get started and that nobody uses inappropriate language. You can also periodically call out their names as if you are a ring announcer. "Ladieeeees and gentlemennnnnn, defending the red corner, we have Bionic Beth." Students will come up with some very creative and memorable names.

In another name game, students make up short stories about the origin of their names, and share these with the class.

Practice names with a ball-toss activity. Stand in a circle and toss a Nerf ball around while calling your own name and the name of the receiver. Pick up the pace as names are learned.

### 6. Quick Interviews and Introductions

Combine students in pairs. Specify three things they are to find out about the other person. (For example, learn the person's middle name and nickname. Find out where the person is in the birth order in his or her family. Find out something they used to be afraid of and something that person is afraid of now. Find out whether or not the person can curl his or her tongue. Find out what historical era that person would visit if they could time travel.) Give them a timed period (about five minutes) to conduct interviews of each other. After the interviews, allow one minute for each student to introduce the partner (to the class) telling some of the things they learned.

### 7. Guess Who?

Students write a list of facts about themselves and then give it to the teacher, who will then read the facts aloud. Students are given ample time to guess who the person is. This is best done after students know each other's names.

## 8. Your Autograph, Please

At the top of a paper, type: *Find someone who:* and then you can write a list of characteristics with a blank beside each item.

Examples:

## May I Have Your Autograph?

Find someone who:

- is left-handed _____
- has green eyes _____
- is wearing tie shoes_____
- has blonde hair _____
- plays the piano _____
- has a birthday in the same month as yours _____
- has a birthday in the month before yours _____
- has a birthday in the month after yours _____
- has visited at least one other country _____
- is using a blue pen to do this assignment _____
- has a pet bird _____
- has been to a professional baseball game _____
- has met a professional athlete or other celebrity _____
- wears braces _____
- can touch his or her nose with own tongue _____
- can pat his or her head while rubbing own belly _____

*Humor in School is Serious Business*

I also try to find a few extra-interesting facts about my students that I could use in this activity. Add a few bonus items such as these, and see what happens.

Examples:

More Autographs

Find someone who:

- has been bitten by a rabid animal _____
- was chased up a tree by a bear _____
- has fallen asleep in a patch of poison ivy _____
- has been bitten by a relative _____
- has tossed his or her lunch in class _____
- has been lunch-tossed-upon in class _____
- has laughed so hard that milk came out of his or her nose

  _____

- has laughed so hard that milk and cookies came out of his

  or her nose _____

- has shouted like Tarzan while swinging from a rope

  _____

Each student has the same sheet and must introduce herself or himself to one other person in the room at a time (including the teacher) and then ask any question from the list. "Is your birthday in April?" If the answer is "Yes," then the other student signs the questioner's paper in the corresponding blank. Any person may sign another person's paper only once, which encourages students to meet pretty much everyone else in the room before the activity is finished. Give students a small prize when their papers are full of autographs.

**9. Personal True-False Tests**

Ask students to create a short true-false test about themselves. Each one takes a turn quizzing the class (or other individuals or small groups) about themselves. They can share correct answers after hearing what others think are the correct answers.

These are just samples of ways to start the year that include humor, fun, and connections with students. Add your own brilliant ideas. These kinds of things—which do, by the way, include **you** cracking smiles before December—let students know that you care about knowing them, and they set the tone for a comfortable, welcoming classroom.

*"Would you mind taking a drink of milk, laughing so hard that it comes out of your nose, then giving me your autograph?"*

## Chapter Summary

- Let them see you smile—OFTEN!

- Ask your students what they want to learn.

- Ask them how they want to learn.

- Put rewards and consequences in place.

- Don't break any laws.

- Let your students get to know you.

- Get to know your students.

- Practice making faces.

- Practice using funny accents.

## Summary of the Summary

- Do good stuff and have fun.

- Don't do bad stuff and don't be mean.

## Summarized Summary of Chapter Summary

Good—yes; bad—no.

*"We decided that this would be a good way to learn geography."*

# 5

## Beg, Borrow, and Embellish to Ban Boredom

Creating a Cheerful,
Humor-Filled Environment

*"Do you think this will be too much of a distraction?"*

One of the 127,362 great things about being a teacher
is that you get to decorate your classroom. I don't know
any other professionals that get to bring as much of their
personalities and interests into the workplace. Most workers
don't have any space to call their own, so there is nothing to
decorate. College professors only get an itsy bitsy 8-foot by
6-foot by 8-foot office space, and most of them fill the 384
cubic feet with outdated textbooks, old rocks, 23 years' worth
of ungraded papers, a lost telephone, an unused computer,
two filing cabinets full of mimeographed tests from the 1970s,
jars of stale peanuts, two thank-you cards (one for actually
helping a student, and one for attending a funeral), a calendar

(often last year's), two chairs (each with a stack of papers from the 1990s), a flag or two, a couple of faded framed degrees, and some mold (which is blamed on the maintenance crew).

Members of the business world can only decorate in a dignified manner or they will "lose the deal." I have surveyed numerous (two) professionals in business and they all say that they must be very careful about the impression made by their décor; it must be of a professional and serious nature.

*Any time that you are out of the house is a chance to be looking for items that might add fun to your classroom décor.*

Professional athletes only get a 3-foot by 2-foot by 6-foot locker to decorate. That's a pretty small space to try to decorate when you are also warehousing your necessary athletic gear like shoes, socks, shorts, steroids, syringes, mysterious powders, shirts, mysterious creams, deodorant, apology-remorse-confession-regret jewelry, towel, semiautomatic handgun, soap, ammunition, skin moisturizer, and a wide variety of "pain-killers."

But teachers . . . teachers get about a whole room (maybe 24 feet by 27 feet by 8 feet) to decorate. I was going to work the cubic footage math for you, but I decided that you needed the practice more than me. It must be right around a whole lot. Whatever the number, fill up all that space with posters, comics, games, activities, fancy borders, and student creations.

As a teacher, any time that you are out of the house is a chance to be looking for items that might add fun to your classroom décor. I taught middle and high school Spanish for 12 years, so every time that I went to a Mexican restaurant or Mexican grocery store, I would ask if they had any posters that I could use in my classroom. I don't recall ever being told, "No." Actually, we were always speaking Spanish, so I should've written, "I don't recall ever being told, 'No.'" Maybe I should explain. The first "No" is in English and the second "No" is in Spanish. Maybe I shouldn't have bothered explaining that. Oh well, it's too late now. Anyway, ask and people will give. Just remember to explain that you are an underpaid, overworked teacher trying to do what is right and best for the children of your community.

## If It Can Be Done Here, It Can Be Done Anywhere

A few years ago, I was hired to teach Spanish at an underprivileged, under-funded, low-socioeconomic level school in Alabama. When I arrived for my first day on the job, I thought that I had entered some sort of detention hall, juvenile delinquent center, or even prison. (I have taken tours of all three and it actually appeared more like a prison than anything else.) The walls were bare and drab except for the encroaching mold, parade of ants marching up and down and all around, and discolored gaps where chunks of cement were missing. The holes in the cement reminded me of the bullet marks left on the prison walls of the maximum-security unit I had visited with a group of at-risk students. (I was the teacher, not an at-risk student, by the way—at least on that occasion.) I knew they were bullet holes because the guards bragged about it to impress me and the students.

Anyway, on this first day of my teaching assignment, I returned to the office to ask if I had found my way to the correct room or if I had accidentally stumbled into "the condemned room of repugnance." The secretary, who doubled as the school nurse, said, "Yessir, that's your room."

I said, "The room is full of ants."

"What?"

"The classroom—it's full of ants. Is there anything we can do about that?"

"I don't know," she replied. "I'll call the custodian and see if he can do anything."

Halfway through my first class, the custodian arrived and sprayed something on the ants. But it didn't help much. They were stunned for a few minutes, but they picked up the pace again and quickly spread their boundaries to avoid the stickiness of the spray. I soon found that if I threw portions of my lunch in the garbage can, I could keep the majority of the nine million ants localized. They would swarm in, on, and around the trash can, fighting each other for my apple core and bread crusts. (I later discovered that the same aforementioned spray was also used as lunchroom disinfectant, bathroom deodorizer, window cleaner, furniture polish, and possibly a breath freshener. I guessed that it was toxic and probably shouldn't be allowed in a school.)

I also asked the custodian if there was anything that we could do to cover the two holes in the wall (big enough to stick an arm through) that went all the way to the outside. He said, "Naw, there ain't nothin' I can do about that now, but anything else you need, just let me know."

Before the custodian could get away, I asked about the exposed electrical wires and open electrical junction box in my classroom. This time he replied, "I don't know nothin' 'bout that now." I should've put my lunch morsels on top of the electrical box so that the ants would have had to climb the exposed wires to get them and then . . . well, the ant problem would have been resolved.

I also asked the secretary-nurse (or nurscretary) why there were no clocks or decorations in the rooms. The nurscretary said that it was because the students just look at them if they put them up in the rooms. Now, if your neighbor brings home a llambra (half llama, half zebra) one day and puts it in his yard, you will probably stare at it for a day or two, but eventually you have to eat a bowl of cereal and get back to your daily activities. If students have never had a clock in their classrooms or colorful, engaging decorations—then of course they stare. They also get back to work when they should.

*Involve your students in the decorating process. Challenge them to contribute ideas that add life, humor, and learning to the classroom.*

One of the first days I was at that school, I brought in a stack of colored paper, as well as colored pens, pencils, and markers. I told my students to make fancy, colorful, and fun labels in Spanish for everything in the classroom. They did. It was fantastic. They labeled everything: light (*la luz*), chalk board (*la pizarra*), walls (*las paredes*), floor (*el piso*), window (*la ventana*), crooked bookcase (*la estantería chueca*), broken desks (*escritorios rotos*), broken chairs (*las sillas rotas*), broken window (*la ventana rota*), holes in the wall (*los hoyos en la pared*), broom (*la escoba*), door (*la puerta*), garbage (*la basura*), ants (*las hormigas*), and me (*el Capitán*). They even made their own paper clock and put it on a wall. Involve your students in the decorating process. Challenge them to contribute ideas that add life, humor, and learning to the classroom. They'll take ownership of the room and the process of making it an inviting place to be. I've found that students come up with some very creative ideas! (I'll share some later in this chapter.)

## Let the Begging Begin

After we had taped all of our labels around the room, we noticed that there were still plenty of bare spaces and holes exposed. So that night I stopped at a local theater and asked to see the manager. I introduced myself as a schoolteacher, and made a nice speech about how leftover movie posters would brighten up my classroom and make the environment more exciting. He said that he wasn't allowed to give away any posters, that they were all to be sent with the movies to the next theater showing the film.

I said, "Oh, that's too bad. My poor students at that underprivileged school will be so disappointed. The school has never been able to afford decorations or paint for the walls. We can't even afford clocks for the classrooms. We don't even have enough money to buy real insecticide, so we just have to teach around the ant infestations. But if you don't have a few posters to spare then I guess we'll make do."

Then I just stood there with a sad-looking smile. After a disturbingly uncomfortable fifty-three seconds of silence, he looked left and looked right and then motioned with his hand to follow. I accompanied him down a dark and forbidding corridor so ominous, bleak, ghastly, and dismal that the blood in my veins ran cold and my knees weakened as I feared for my life. Not really, but it was kind of darkish until my eyes adjusted. I wondered if he was taking me to a soundproof room in the back to give me a stern talking-to away from the

> Do whatever it takes to bring life and cheer to students' surroundings.

paying customers, or if he was going to beat me up.

I was right. He led me to a back storage area with foam-padded walls. I thought, "Okay, it's go time," so I held both fists out in front of me in a classic 1893 posed boxing stance—arms extended, fists clinched, body turned one-eighth circle to the right, and the head held back. I added my own scaredy-cat squint and chewed on the right side of my lower lip. Then he started loading rolled-up posters hastily into my waiting arms. When I had so many posters that I could barely carry them and hardly see over the top, he opened the door from the storage room, peeked left and right, and then said, "If you ever want to bring your students in for a matinee, I'll show them something for free and give them each a drink and popcorn."

Then he led me down a different dark hallway and shoved me out a back door with a "Don't tell anybody about this," and all of a sudden I was in a dark alley leading to the parking lot. I felt like I was committing a misdemeanor. I started to run (actually, trot very slowly) and the posters began falling. The more I tried to catch them the more they fell. I decided to run in serpentine fashion, just in case the Hollywood cops were on the lookout and wanted to take a shot at an illegal poster pilferer. (I have been told that it is more difficult to shoot someone who is running serpentine rather than a straight line.) I threw the posters in my truck and then serpentined back to pick up those that had fallen. I guess the moral of this story is: Never be afraid to look pitiful for a good cause.

I was excited on my drive to school the next day. We could now decorate with posters and label them in Spanish. When

I opened the door to my classroom, I couldn't believe what I saw. All of our signs were strewn over the floor. Was a student mad at me and thought this was a way of getting revenge? Was a teacher jealous that I was decorating my classroom when nobody else was? Were the ants messing with me? I began slowly putting them back in place. I was about two minutes into this activity when they all began falling down again. The walls were so greasy and dirty that nothing would stick.

Keep this in mind: You might have to wash the walls before you can start to spice things up! If that's what it takes, roll up your sleeves. That's what we did—as a group. We washed the walls and then redecorated. Students laughed and laughed as they commented on each other's artwork and put the room together with posters, labels, fake clock, and some original works of art. They also made comic strip-type talk bubbles coming out of the mouths of many of the people on the posters. They enjoyed making up little remarks in Spanish that these actors might say.

## Beg More; Then Embellish

Every city has numerous places of business that can and will supply teachers with posters and other decorations that relate to your chapters, units, and subject areas, and when displayed they will brighten classrooms and attitudes. Most of the posters that I collect from restaurants, grocery stores, theaters, and other businesses display people interacting, playing, working, or selling a product. I'll tie that previous sentence together with the rest of this paragraph in a few minutes, but for now it will seem that I have lost my train of thought. I actually do lose my train of thought quite often, but not this time. This time I'm staying focused. (*Hmm . . . I was just thinking what a funny word "train" is. Choo-choo train,*

*train for athletics, educational training, part of a bridal dress, train animals to . . . uh oh.*) Sorry, that wasn't very professional of me. Let's get back on the bus, or maybe I should say let's get back on the train . . . Auugh, just get to the point.

At every school where I have taught, the teachers line up with their students on photo day and get their pictures taken for the yearbook. Then a couple of weeks later, the teachers are given a free packet of pictures of themselves. For a few years, I wondered what I would do with all of those gigantic, large, medium, and wallet-sized photographs of myself that

were rapidly accumulating. It no longer seemed cool to send posed school photographs of myself to friends and relatives. What would I say? "I thought you might like to see how much I've grown between ages thirty-eight and thirty-nine." or "My mom and dad are very proud of me for not getting into any fights this year." or "I still don't like celery, but I can eat squash now without throwing up in my mouth." Also, none of my friends in their 30s and 40s have wallet-sized photos of themselves to trade with me. Anyway, I decided to transpose my pictures onto the faces on the posters. The students loved it—and the posters served as great motivators for writing sentences, stories, or dramas. See how nicely that all eventually tied together?

I got to school extra early on the morning that the school photographs were to be delivered. While retrieving my packet from my mailbox, I thought, "Hmm, maybe the head football coach's picture would look cool on my SPAM poster. And maybe the basketball coach would look great playing the piano, and the history teacher peddling piña-flavored soda, and the principal skateboarding with a candy bar, and the entire male science department running a race . . . shirtless." So I hurriedly grabbed all of the teacher photo packets and ran to my room and went to work like Edward Scissorhands. With a pair of scissors and a ton of trimming, all of the heads fit perfectly. I cut out 12 of my own heads with all of my different hairstyles over the years, and put them on the Olympic basketball dream team poster. Students laughed and looked closely at each individual poster.

Whenever I perform those selfless acts of kindness (i.e. waste time for the sake of humor), teachers tend to ask me questions like, "How do you have time to do things like that?" and "Don't you have anything better to do with your time?"

To the first question I say, "I make time. I wake up early and I don't watch more than two hours of TV per week."

To the second question I say, "No. There are a ton of things that I would **like** to be doing (running, golfing, fishing, working on or driving my 1967 Plymouth Barracuda or my 1963 Plymouth Valiant convertible, running, playing basketball, playing Nerf basketball, running, playing catch, playing UNO, shooting BB guns, running, shooting bow and arrows, riding our go-cart, riding bicycles, or even running), but right now this is more important."

By the way, those posters also offer great target language questioning and discussion. I can just point and ask: "¿Al señor Robusto, que le gusta beber?" ("What does Mr. Robusto like to drink?") "¿Al director, que le gusta hacer?" ("What does the principal like to do?") Teachers and students visit my room often to see whose pictures have been added where.

*Your chronic daydreamers or wall-starers will learn more if you give them something funny and informational to view.*

## Get Students in on the Embellishing

Students enjoy changing classroom décor often. It's a good way to introduce the upcoming chapter or unit, and students learn while they make, create, and decorate. Students who make the signs, color the pictures, look at vocabulary to be used with the new topic, and laugh while doing it will already have learned some of the information before you start the unit. I've also found that the chronic daydreamers or wall-starers (close enough to being a real word) will learn more if you give them something fun and informational to view. Sometimes I even ask questions on a test that deal with posters or vocabulary in the room, just to see who has noticed.

Students do a great job decorating and they make the room feel fun and inviting. For eight years, I taught in a classroom without windows. One year, a student brought in blinds and curtains, and we made our own windows. Students even painted a nice scene behind the blinds. Another year, we even put up a door in the back corner of the room. It only opened up to the wall, but it made people wonder— and the principal even checked more than once to see if it went anywhere. Students thought it was hilarious to trick the principal.

Make sure to include plenty of student work and creations in classroom décor. I held a piñata contest each year and hung the piñatas from the classroom ceiling for weeks to follow. They were colorful, pleasing to look at, and reminded us of the fun times we had constructing them together. (Be sure to make use of your ceilings!)

*When students help to create the humorous environment, they are not likely to deface, disrespect, or destroy it.*

Students also enjoy putting the comic strip-type talk balloons with little quote sayings coming from their teachers' mouths on the posters. "A mi me gusta comer la SPAM." "Yo no toco el piano muy bien." We can easily change the sayings to match each chapter or grammar lesson.

I always leave one bulletin board open for the posting of comic strips that are related to the foreign language or other subject being taught. For the most part, students bring in all of them and post them. It is just one more way of encouraging them to pay attention to their surroundings and the use of language. Students can often be found reading the comic strips on the board before and after class. They voluntarily struggle to figure something out if there is a chance that they might laugh.

I also provide an empty message board for students to leave fun messages for each other. The only stipulation is that they have to use Spanish. I was told by other teachers that students would abuse the privilege and write vulgar things. They never do. When students help to create the humorous environment, they enjoy the classroom more and are not likely to deface, disrespect, or destroy it. The posters, talk balloons with little sayings, message boards, etc., can all be adjusted to meet your own age groups and subject areas.

## Borrow

This story will give you some ideas for things you might want to try, after you have secured a tenured position. The purpose is to encourage you to look around and see what you might borrow to add life and laughter to your classroom. My wife's aunt sent her an 18-inch, fully functional, teddy bear telephone for Christmas. It had a small push-button panel on its belly. Other than that, it looked and felt just like a great big teddy bear. Okay, it also had a phone cord coming out of its rear end, but if you were to look at it from the front, you probably would not see that.

That this gift came into our hands was a blessing. I had grown tired of answering the phone calls from the office to my classroom at inopportune times. Classroom phones are always as far away as possible from a convenient spot in the room, delaying my arrival and subsequent "Hola" by three or four extra rings. The students, now distracted and disturbed, just have to know who it was, what she or he wanted, why she or he called now, and why they (the students) couldn't answer the phone themselves. Each individual phone call is nothing more than a minor disturbance, but collectively, such calls add up to a lot of wasted time and energy in the classroom.

Usually a phone call to my classroom results in a conversation of this sort:

"Hola, Buenos días."

"Hello, Mr. Hurren, is that you?"

"Hang on a second, let me check my name tag. Sí, soy yo. Yes, it is I."

Pause. "I, what?"

"Sorry, I'm using correct grammar. Yes, this is Mr. Hurren."

"Oh, okay, this is Vice Principal, Mr. Reynerd. I wanted to know if you had the list of track team members."

"Yes."

"Could you give them to me after school?"

"The team members or the list?"

"The list."

"Yes."

"Okay, then. You can just put them in my box if I'm not here."

"The team members or the list?"

Pause. "The list."

"Oh, okay."

"Good-bye."

"Adios."

One time I asked, "Did you really need to disturb my class for this?"

He responded, "Sorry, but yes I did. I need that form by the end of the week."

I said, "If it's not an emergency, couldn't you just send me an e-mail?" But then I started getting e-mails **and** phone calls for everything. I guess that served me right for asking questions.

It is this sort of nonsensical waste of time (which occurs between 3 and 143 times per day) that irritates me. Just ask me personally, already! I'm always at my door in between classes. Or just put a little note in my box or send me an e-mail, but don't waste valuable class time with blather—because whatever time is wasted, it's doubled in order to refocus the students. But, as usual, I found my own way to enjoy the situation instead of letting it frustrate and anger me.

Back to the teddy bear phone that I described all too many paragraphs ago—remember?—the one that belonged to my wife? Well, its niftiest features are these: It is a speaker phone, and its mouth and eyes move as the caller speaks. So I "borrowed" that phone for a while. I spent the better part of an evening taking apart the classroom wall clock and phone unit, rewiring the system, running new wires through the ceiling of my classroom and down to a desk in the middle of the room where I connected the bear phone. My wall clock was mounted at a permanent slant after that, but it added to the décor of the room. Now when someone called, I could immediately signal a student to hit the "on" button and I could holler, "Halo." I know some of you are thinking that I misspelled "Hola," but I didn't. I wanted to write "Halo." It is more fun to yell "Halo" than "Hola." (If you want to try it, just remember that in Spanish the letter "h" is silent.)

Now I wouldn't have to waste time walking to the far corner of the room, nor would I have to waste time getting students back on task. Because they had already heard the conversation, nobody was curious. And it's a real hoot to watch the teddy bear mouth the words and roll his eyes throughout the conversation. I figured the phone and the caller already disturbed us, so we might as well have some fun with it and then move on with our work. With this new system, my conversations with the teddy bear phone proceeded something like this:

Click. "¡Halo!"

"Umm, Mr. Hurren?"

> Numerous teachers came to me to ask, "What did you do now, Lee?"

*Humor in School is Serious Business*

"Sí."

"Is that you, Mr. Hurren?"

"Yes, it is I, Mr. B. Lee Hurren. Who are you?"

"It doesn't sound like you." (Stifled laughter from my students at the comment and the bear moving its mouth and rolling its eyes.)

"Well, I look like me." More stifled giggles. "Who are you?"

"This is Coach Hakalarious. Send Chris to see me."

"Oh, the football coach. Hey, when are we going to win a game?"

"Just send Chris over here."

"Is it related to academics?"

"Just send Chris to me."

"Soooooo, you want me to send Chris to see you for something non-school related, is that correct?"

"Yeah."

"This may sound weird to you, but during class time I try to do learning stuff and right now we're in the middle of something that is kind of learningish oriented. Can he come at another time?"

"No, I need to see him about his uniform."

"Oh, well, I didn't know it was that kind of an emergency. I'll send him right away. Hey, how's the amnesia?"

"What?"

"That bad, huh? All righty, Chris is on his way to clear up the uniform emergency. Adiós Teddy, I mean Davey."

I'm sure some of you are saying, "Now **you're** wasting even more time than before." And my comment to that is . . . "He started it." Instantly, instead of feeling frustrated, I started looking forward to receiving phone calls, and when they came I would keep the caller on the line as long as possible. It was great entertainment, and after the laughter, we'd get right back to work—seemingly better than before.

But eventually word got around to the principal, so he put a note in everyone's box that said, "Teachers, there are no foreign electronics allowed in your classrooms. If you have installed any without authorization, they are to be removed immediately." He also read it over the loud speaker during announcement time. My students laughed. And as usual, when we received notes like this, numerous teachers came to me to ask, "What did you do now, Lee?"

I knew what the principal meant by "foreign electronics" (anything not issued by the school district), but I still had to check in front of the students. I lifted up Teddy and sure enough, it read "Made in Taiwan." A few weeks later, I found an answering machine that had "Made in USA" stamped on the back. I wired that into the system and recorded the following message: "Halo . . . Halo . . . Halo? . . . Halooooooo. Oh, whoopsiedaisy, I'm sorry. . . I guess you're talking to el Capitán's answering machine. I must be in the middle of teaching to the standardized tests that we're required to give. If you will leave your name and number after the beep, I'll call you back as soon as you are busy or as soon as all students everywhere are above average, whichever comes first. Gracias. Beep." After each call there would generally be a long pause and then . . . click. It was a great timesaver and a lot of fun, too.

I never got to try other messages, because all too soon there was another note in our boxes and an announcement by the principal that read, "Teachers, telephone answering machines are not allowed in the classroom." Oh well, it gave me a few more curious visitors for a few days.

You can have fun with all sorts of borrowed items. Be on the lookout for them. Maybe use them for more educational purposes than I used the teddy bear phone, though. Always be thinking, "How can I use this item to teach something in a way that my students will remember it?"

## Embellish Some More

You can find great items to use in the classroom at such places as the dollar stores (Dollar Tree, Dollar General, Dollar Colonel, Dollar Private First Class, 99 Cents or Less), discount stores, vintage stores, Salvation Army or Goodwill stores, yard sales, Oriental Trading Company, and Teacher's Discovery. When you order something from Teacher's Discovery, they send you an I.D. card that looks like a credit card and it has **Discovery** spelled out in large letters on it. I used to like to ask merchants if they accept the Discover . . . y card. They would always say, "yes," and then I would hand them my bright yellow Teacher's Discovery card. I decided to stop doing that after my wife said, "Stop doing that, NOW," and after spending a few weeks in jail for credit card fraud. (Not really.)

*Don't let the visual or intellectual stimulation get stale. Change the look and content of your room décor often.*

Don't let the visual or intellectual stimulation get stale. Change the look and content of your room décor often. It keeps the atmosphere fresh and fun. You can redesign with each new unit or chapter, or coordinate with each approaching holiday. Just remember to get student input and assistance. And **always** include humor.

## Beg Perpetually

One last story for this chapter: I was with my wife and children at a Halloween carnival one year and somebody had made a fantastic indoor (almost portable) miniature golf course. It was a two-hole version of a putt-putt course. After my children (and I) had played it a few times, I asked the ticket-taker how he made it. He gave me a 20-minute description of which I understood 45 seconds worth, so I went into my bobble-head mode, nodding my head up and down while saying, "Yep, yep, yep" every minute or so. When he was done explaining, there was an awkward silence, because I didn't know what to say or how to say it (Is it possible to not know how to say nothing?), so I just asked, "What are you going to do with it when this is over?"

He said, "After tomorrow, it goes in the trash."

I gasped, "What?"

He replied, "Yep."

I said, "I wish I could fit this thing in my truck. I'd take it to school with me. My students would love this as a bonus activity for excellent work."

He stared at me. "You're a school teacher?"

"Yessir."

"Don't look like no school teacher."

"Well, I teach Spanish." I don't know why that made my looks more acceptable, but it did. He said that he would

*"I'm a teacher."*

deliver it to me at school and he did. It folded up against the wall, and we could move back some desks to use it on the floor. We used it for review games and extra credit chances. It was a great addition to the classroom.

Beg for used CDs and hang them from the ceiling with fishing line. All of those free CDs that come in the mail can finally be put to use (they are also great BB gun targets—but not in school). I know some teachers who hang student work and other fun stuff from clamp-type clothespins that are tied to the ceiling with fishing line. This makes it quick and easy to change and redecorate. Others use thin sheets of colored cellophane paper to cover the lights in their classrooms and effectively change the mood. (Check the fire codes before doing this.) Each chapter, unit, or new season can and should be reason enough to celebrate with new decorations in the classroom.

If you're a teacher, get used to the idea that you have got to learn to beg, borrow, and almost steal (note the "almost") to make your classroom better for your students. You never know until you ask.

## Chapter Summary

- Have fun decorating.

- Get students involved so they will take ownership of the classroom.

- Let students take charge of a bulletin board.

- Change room décor often.

- Be daring (in a safe way).

- Include jokes, cartoons, funny faces, and other humor in the décor.

- Include humorous stuff that teaches or reviews content.

- Ask questions on tests and quizzes about decorations.

- Make up sayings from and for your posters.

- Ask and people will give. Never be afraid to beg.

- Look sad and grief-stricken and they will give more.

- Find stuff at dollar stores, thrift stores, restaurants, grocery stores, clothing stores, yard sales, your attic, other people's attics and garages, students' parents, and partners-in-education. And, ask around.

## Summary of the Summary

- Involve students wisely and funnily (look it up) while decorating.

- Borrow and beg for stuff. Embellish what you get.

## Combined Summary of Chapter Summary

Beg, borrow, and embellish. Get students to do this, too.

# 6

## A Group Guffaw Gets Things Goin'

### Starting the Day

*"If you know of a better way to jump-start their brains, I'm all ears."*

What irony! I can't figure out how to start this chapter that is supposed to be all about how to start the day with humor. Hmm, wow, I'm really stumped here. Oh well, I gave it my best shot. Maybe I'll just skip this chapter and let you start the day however you want. Just say something funny and then start teaching; that ought to work fine. I'm sure that some of you will be kind of disappointed in this chapter, but I did put a lot of effort into the first five chapters (maybe just four of the five), and I'll try much harder with Chapter 7. I'm sorry, but I'm just not feeling anything.

Okay, I'm back. I think I've identified my problems with this chapter. First of all, it's the first chapter that I've had to write under contract. Now that I've actually been granted a deal for this book, I've lost my creative edge. I used to investigate humor and do crazy-fun things because of the love and passion for it. But now—now I'm a professional. I get paid to do this. It's no longer fun; it's a job. Well, I quit. *Note to publisher: Not really. I need the money. I'm just trying to trick myself into being creative again.*

And secondly, this chapter really isn't that exciting. As I said before, just start class with a joke or a funny story. There, now I'm done.

Oh great, I just got a call from my editor and she said that we need more material and information for this chapter or the deal is off. I said, "I'm a professional writer and I know what's best for my readers."

She responded with, "At this point there are no readers, and how can you consider yourself a professional when you haven't sold a single copy of your book yet?"

I shot back with, "If you want more, then maybe you should write it yourself."

She answered, "Maybe I will, because it seems to me that anybody can write this drivel that I have in front of me right now."

So, I'm writing again.

## A Jump-Start and a Soft Heart

I doubt that any of you have ever had a class in college that taught you how to start class with a joke. Yet it just might be the most effective way to get your students' attention and let them know that you care about them. When it's the first class of the day, the students are coming to you with the feeling that it's entirely your fault that they even have to be there. And remember, for them the school day often is not pleasant. All of your students have experienced any one, or any combination of the following before even arriving to your first-period class:

1. Woke up late

2. Missed breakfast

3. Had to eat plain oatmeal because they were out of pop-tarts

4. Missed the bus

5. Got yelled at by parents

6. Got yelled at by siblings

7. Got yelled at by bus driver

8. Forgot homework

9. Lost homework

10. Homework was destroyed by a natural disaster

11. Lunch money was stolen

12. Tripped on the bus

13. Got laughed at on the bus

14. Lost favorite shoes

15. Favorite team logo shirt was dirty—so dirty that not even a middle school student would wear it

16. Bad hair day

17. Got tripped in the hall

18. Dropped books in the hall

19. Forgot locker combination

20. Pet goldfish died and had to be flushed down the toilet last night

And all of that is your fault. If it weren't for you, they could all have slept in until noon and never had to worry about anything.

*"I bet this is our biology teacher's fault."*

If your class is at any other time of the day than the first thing in the morning, then many of your students are arriving to your classroom feeling mean and hateful, and not wanting to be in your class for any one, or any combination of the following reasons:

1. Previous teacher was mean

2. Previous teacher yelled at him or her

3. Previous teacher is lousy

4. Previous teacher is boring

5. Previous teacher wears the same clothes everyday

6. Previous teacher has terrible breath

7. Previous teacher has terrible breath and yelled a lot

8. Previous teacher assigned tons of homework

9. Previous teacher thinks she or he is the only teacher in the whole school who assigns homework

10. Previous teacher gave an awful exam

11. Previous teacher gave a pop quiz—unexpected, of course (Isn't that what pop quizzes are?)

12. Previous teacher made students write an essay of 1,000 words on how to behave in class

13. Lunch was lousy

14. Lunch spilled

15. Forgot lunch

16. Forgot lunch money

17. Was dumped just before lunch by boyfriend (or girlfriend)

18. Was bullied at lunch

19. Was punished with silent lunch

20. Sat at assembly next to student with terrible body odor

21. Broke pencil tip, got up to sharpen pencil, got in trouble for being out of seat, and see #12

22. Copied notes nonstop for 57 minutes from projected presentation

23. Was tardy to another class by 3 seconds, got locked out of classroom by teacher, had to go to office and wait to see principal to get a permission slip to get back into class before teacher would unlock door, finally got permission slip, went back to class for last 11 minutes, had to stay after class to explain actions to teacher and apologize . . . "like you mean it," which caused the student to arrive late to your class while muttering "I hate school. I wish I had never come today. I can't wait until I can drop out of this loserville."

24. Forgot to put pants back on after P.E. class

And some of them do drop out. So what are you going to do about it? Huh? Did anybody in your expensive college classes teach you how to handle that? Oh yeah, I know. Your professors taught you to get to know each student individually and to be able to quickly and skillfully recognize any and every student who may need individual attention. Then what? Don't get me wrong; I use as many of the proven, research-based effective teaching strategies as possible. But sometimes all the class needs is a little bit of humor and then we're all ready to move forward with refreshed feelings, reinvigorated minds, and smiles on our faces.

## Students Need a Fresh Start—Every Day

Humor may not cure every aforementioned woe every time, but it goes a long way toward alleviating lots of pain—and maybe it does cure many of the ills. As for the coffee breath, only a combination of brushing, mouthwash, tongue scraping, mint gum, breath mints, vitamin C, baking soda, hydrogen peroxide, and guava will help. If those don't work, then maybe kerosene and a flame-thrower will. It's an amazing thing—kerosene. No, I mean humor—how starting class with a joke, a humorous anecdote, or a funny cartoon puts everybody at ease, gives us all something in common to giggle about, and allows us to all start anew. The shared laugh or chuckle, or even a chortle, seems to unite the class. I know it sounds a little over-glorified, but it works.

The first time I consciously started class with humor was when I heard one of my 7th-grader's declarations from my 6th period as he arrived to my classroom (5th door on the left) during the 4th day of the 3rd week of the 2nd month of my 1st year of teaching. (Wow, what a memory!) That student came into my classroom, slammed down his books, let out a long audible grunt, and said, "I can't stand Mr. Bellows. All he does is yell at us all day and then pile on the homework. We don't even know how to do any of this stuff. He doesn't teach us anything." And then a bunch of other students joined in.

> Humor may not cure every woe students bring to class every time, but it goes a long way toward alleviating lots of pain.

"Yeah, he doesn't even know what he's talking about."

"I wish I could take any other class instead of that."

"I've tried to get my parents to move to another school zone just so I wouldn't have to take Mr. Bellows."

"Yeah."

"Yeah."

"Me, too."

"Uh huh."

"Yep."

"You got that right."

And I seem to remember somebody saying, "Your tie doesn't match anything you're wearing today," but that doesn't really add to the story. All of this happened in an instant. Students were mad and I needed to do something, because they certainly weren't thinking about Spanish class, nor did they **want** to think about it. So I sprang into action. (Or is it sprung into action? Springed into action? Spranged into action? Sproinged into action?)

Anyway, I thought quickly and went with the following: I called a student up to the front of the room and I quickly grabbed my water bottle and said, "All right, tell me in Spanish how you feel about Mr. Bellows' class." I took a drink.

He said, "Señor Bellows es un bruto."

I spewed my water all over the floor and looked in disgust at the students. They roared with laughter. I asked a girl in the second row to say in Spanish, "I don't like Mr. Bellows' class."

She said, "No me gusto señor Bellows' clase."

I coughed and gagged out another mouthful of water.

*Humor in School is Serious Business*

More laughter. And finally, I asked the boy who started all of this to say in Spanish, "I want to be just like Mr. Bellows."

He said, "No way, man."

I screamed, "SAY IT!!!" More laughter.

"Yo quiero ser señor Bellows."

I let water just dribble out of my mouth, onto my shirt and unmatching tie, and onto the floor. More laughter.

Then somebody in the front row said, "See what I mean? Why can't more teachers be like you Capitán Hurren?"

To which I responded, "Because I'm the best thing since sliced bread."

No, I didn't say that. I said something like, "Because if they were, this whole school would be headed down the loo." They laughed again. Make no mistake about all of the laughter at this point. I'm sure you've noticed that none of the aforementioned stuff is super funny. In fact, some of you have probably gotten bored and quit reading. But the students laughed because the water gags were unexpected, as were the solicitations.

Then we went to work. I told them that we would need to get the previous three statements correct. So we worked on the chalkboard (yes, chalkboard; it was a low-budget middle school in a very poor area of Nevada) and on paper until we got them grammatically correct.

> The class started out with students feeling terrible and emotions running high. With a little humor, they ended up having a great time, paying careful attention, and learning something useful.

The class started out with kids feeling terrible and emotions running high. With a little humor, they ended up having a great time, paying careful attention, and learning something useful—new grammar that was meaningful. After all, it was their topic that we dealt with that day. I won't give all of you readers the grammar lessons, but we ended up with, "El señor Bellows es un bruto," "No me gusta la clase del señor Bellows," and "Yo quiero ser exactamente como el señor Bellows." (By the way, whenever I talk about other teachers in my class, I always make my students promise that if they ever tell anybody I will personally see to it that they never graduate from middle school, high school, driver's ed., or Harvard Law School. I will also pay a visit to tell that teacher we were talking about him or her, but I don't always say why. Use your good judgment on this—if you have such a thing.)

Hopefully, your students don't come into your classroom griping and complaining about other teachers on a regular basis. But the lesson I learned that day was that a little bit of humor goes a long way. So if we can plan on starting our classes with a little joke, story or comic, we will capture students' attention, relieve some stress, and be better able to move forward with our lessons. Something else happens: the anger (in this case at another teacher) gets diffused. Students don't feel as annoyed anymore because the hostile emotion was turned into something fun and productive. They really are less likely to keep complaining as loudly about that teacher or about any other irritation.

## Collections and Preparations for a Fun Kickoff

Keep files of short jokes, stories, cartoons, and comic strips that you might want to use in class. Be prepared to project or otherwise display cartoons, comic strips, and other funny images—because it's fun for students to see the drawings, too.

When you hear or read a joke that makes you laugh or giggle, write it down. Chances are, if you laughed, so will others. Just make sure that it's appropriate and doesn't fall into any of the categories to avoid. (See Chapter 18.) You can also find jokes-of-the-day on the Internet and a myriad of websites that are full of jokes for specific topics. Keep the appropriate ones in files to use as needed.

Share funny personal stories. Before beginning a chapter on travel, I start the day with this story about my first international flight: When I landed in Chile, at age 19, I was greeted by an airport guard who was holding a machine gun. As he turned to greet me, the barrel of the gun pointed up my nose and he said, "¿De dónde eres?" But he said it very quickly and with a Chileno accent. I knew those three words, but I had only heard them as "¿Deeeeeeeeeeeeeee dooooooooooonnnnnnndeeeeeeeeeeee eeeeeeeeereeeeeeeeeeeeeeeeeeeeeessssssssssss?"

I stared down the barrel of that machine gun (made a scared face here), panicked, and raised both of my arms into the international sign for "I surrender." He laughed and said, "¿Deeeeeeeeeeeeeee dooooooooooonnnnnnndeeeeeeeeeeee eeeeeeeeereeeeeeeeeeeeeeeeeeeeeessssssssssss?"

Still in panic mode and now fearing that his laughter could set off the hairpin trigger on his fully-automatic machine gun (made a super scared face here), I lost all use of my limited Spanish training and replied, "El avión." Yep, your half-witted teacher is from the airplane. Born and raised on an airplane—that is who I am. That is also why I am so dimwitted that I can't even answer a simple question like that. The guard laughed even harder and then fired a few warning shots over my head and told me to never come back to his airport. My students laugh pretty hard at (with) their teacher, and then I make it clear that no shots were fired, because I don't want the students thinking that I was shot at with a machine gun, even though I might be perceived as slightly heroic instead of a goofball. At this point the students are all more excited to learn a little more about how to get through an airport in a Spanish-speaking country, knowing that their teacher barely made it on his first attempt.

You can also use tricks to start class. I'm not a magician, but I have allowed a few students to show magic tricks, yo-yo tricks, and even those silly finger-skateboard tricks. They get students' attention, allow them to misremember (love that word) any lingering negative feelings, and away we go to learning.

A snack now and then complements humor nicely. When you can afford it (and if school policies allow), mix your opening joke with a platter of donuts (or something healthy like tofu-tuna-sprout cookies and guava-seaweed juice).

## Start-up Humor Minus the Mayhem

Some people ask me, "But doesn't all mayhem break loose in your classroom after you do something like that?"

The answer is long and complicated with a lot of research, details, resources, personal examples, and experiences. So hang in there with me as I explain it. It goes something like this: "No."

I guess there is an explanation that is just a little bit longer. As long as we are all clear about the time frame for jokes, comics, tricks, and stories, students know their boundaries and limits (usually). Every once in a while, I have to quiet them down and remind them that we will be back again tomorrow and somebody else can share something then.

Don't be afraid to allow students to participate in the sharing of stories and jokes. They must adhere to my (your) rules of "no offensive humor," etc., and I let them know that if they don't, we will put an end to it. In my many years of teaching, only a few jokes were even questionable. For those, I simply reminded students that if anything might be questionable, they had better preapprove it with me or not use it.

I will end this chapter by sharing my favorite joke as told by one of my students. (We teachers need a good chuckle once in a while, too.)

A rich man who lived at the top of a big hill was carrying his groceries into his house when a bag burst, spilling his food. At the same time, a poor man at the bottom of the hill had gone in search of his next meal. Being unsuccessful, he decided to pray for food. While praying, he was hit in the side of the head with a big wheel of cheese. He ran home, slammed the door shut and demanded that his wife make nachos. She asked, "Wouldn't you rather have enchiladas?"

The poor man replied, "No, we must have nachos, because as I was praying for food I got hit in the side of the head by this cheese and when I picked it up and started to run for home, I could hear a voice from above shouting, 'That's not-yo' cheese, that's not-yo' cheese.'"

## Chapter Summary

- Money is not a good motivator for creativity.

- Publishers don't like to be told, "Write it yourself."

- Students come to class with a lot of problems.

- Many college courses do a lousy job of preparing you for the reality stated in the point just above this one.

- A lot of teachers have bad breath.

- Humor and laughter help students forget their problems and rejuvenate for your class.

- Donuts are better than sliced bread.

- Keep files of jokes, comics, and funny stories.

- Don't try to make someone laugh who is pointing a loaded, fully-automatic weapon at you.

- Nacho cheese is great with tortilla chips.

## Summary of the Summary

Start the day with humor and donuts. Both go a long way toward waking students up; relieving the apathy, tensions, disappointments, hostilities, and other problems they bring to class; and getting them ready to learn.

# 7

## Sillybuses and Such

### Fun with Course Outlines and Other Forms

*"It says we're going to battle against the forces of ignorance."*

Not all of you will be required to generate a syllabus to distribute to students. But let me heartily recommend that you do it anyway. After all, you will be creating some document for yourself anyway that has an overview of your course—right? And students deserve to know what the class is all about, too. A course outline or syllabus is a good way to let kids in on what it is they'll learn. They might even be impressed, or—better yet, excited! So a syllabus is a good thing to create. But this chapter isn't just about the course outline. Its purpose is to help you be more creative and humorous when developing study guides, written assignments, or any other additional paperwork or forms for students, parents, and other educational partners. Syllabi and other prepared forms are safe and easy ways to share some humor and let others know that your class is a fun place to be.

By the way, isn't *syllabi* a cool word? As soon as most people learn it, they start overusing it. Or at least I do. I tell my students this: "My syllabi can be found online, whereas my syllabi used to appear only in hard-copy syllabi form. But now that paper is in short supply for syllabi, I have created my syllabi in electronic format so that you can examine my syllabi and download my syllabi and forward my syllabi and view my syllabi . . ." We (I) overuse *syllabi* so much that we don't even realize that *syllabus* and *syllabuses* are real words. *(I need to have someone call me every ten minutes while I'm writing this book and keep me on track. With my divergent mind, I'm always getting myself sidetracked.)*

Speaking of divergence: Recently, at an educational conference, I attended a session called "The Divergent Learner in the Classroom." I assumed that I would learn how to help those students that are like me, but instead the presenter spent ninety minutes of our lives (that we will never get back) telling us how and why the divergent learner is really just an underachiever. I hope this book sells forty-three million copies, so that I can slam it down on his desk and say, "Aha! This was written by an underachiever."

He'll probably just say very casually, "Just think of how good it would've been had you applied yourself."

## Spice Up Those Syllabuses

Sorry for getting sidetracked. When I create a course outline, like most of you, I start with the name of the class and the year. After this, I put my name and my titles; fake and real. Attorneys and members of the medical profession always have a bunch of letters and titles after their names and now, so do I. I don't know what all the letters mean, so why should anyone care about mine—other than that it looks impressive? My own education, combined with my time teaching in school makes

*"I got a note from my doctor to transfer to Mr. Harding's English class, because it's 100% natural and organic."*

44 years of education, so I deserve a few titles. (I reached the number 44 by counting two years for each year that I was teaching and going to school; I think that's fair. I don't want you to think I am older than I really am.)

After my name, I often put "divergent learner" (D.L.) and "caffeine free" (C.F.). I want my students to know that, as a student, I may not be the greatest "payer-attentioner" (or "knower of vocabulary words") in the world, but that I've worked hard and stuck with education and had some success—thus the labels H.W. (hard worker) and Ph.D. (Kids can imagine what this means.) And I want them to know that I've done it all without the assistance of performance-enhancing drugs. So I make up whatever acronyms and abbreviations I like to put after my name, such as N.H.O.P.E.D.E.U. (no hallucinogenic or performance-enhancing drugs ever used). I've also used many of the following acronyms and helped other teachers use some that didn't make any sense for me to use, but might fit their subject areas. Remember, you can use comments and titles like these on papers other than just a *syllabuster*. They help convey the message that you enjoy what you are doing.

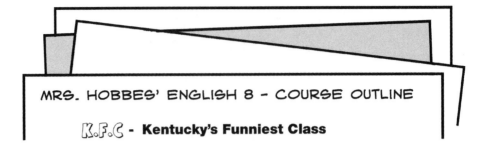

## MRS. HOBBES' ENGLISH 8 - COURSE OUTLINE

### K.F.C - Kentucky's Funniest Class

- ESPN Every Student's Personal Nightmare
- TNT Teacher Not Therapist (Thespian)
- MMA Master Math Advocate
- CBS Certified Best Spanish
- NCLB No Chocolate Left Behind
- NASCAR National Advancement of Spanish (or Science) And Running (or Research)
- NBA National Biology (Bullfighting) Association
- NFL National Fun Laboratory
- NHL National Humor Laboratory
- MLB Major League Biology
- AMA Attractive Math Advocate
- HBO Hyperactive Body Odor
- NBC Number 1 Biology Class
- ABC Adroit Business Class
- IHOP International House of Physics
- PGA Preferred Geometry Ally

## Sell Your Class to Students

Watch (or listen to) more commercials. Here are two other good ways to gather ideas for selling your class to students: Go shopping more. Watch more TV. Then you can use the same great marketing schemes that have sold millions and millions of mediocre and sub-par products for decades. Use the same buzzwords and phrases that they are using. Below is a sampling of examples that I have used in my "Course Description" and "Contents" sections on my syllabibuses (I couldn't choose which plural to use) and some of them are even pertinent to my classes—or to me. You can also use these on other papers, assignments, letters to parents, study guides, homework review sheets, and such.

- This class is a **smart choice**.

- Everything that we do in this class will be **fat free**, except when we go to the kitchen and cook and eat a bunch of fattening tacos, enchiladas, molé, burritos, and quesadillas.

- By the end of the semester, your brain will be **double size**.

- It's **twice as crunchy** as the leading English class.

- All assignments are **100% natural**, except for the crunchy parts.

- 80% of homework is **guaranteed chewy**.

- This textbook is **crispy on the outside and gooey on the inside**.

- **Low-fat** reading assignments.

- **Peanut buttery**.

- **Made in the USA**.

- Puede contener rastros de almendra. (Sorry, wrong side of the box.)

- **Excellent choice, according to Oprah.**

- **Official class of** the Professional Golfers' Association.

- **Soothing** lectures.

- **Replenishes**.

- Carrying the textbook **revitalizes 25% of all muscle groups**.

- **Quick absorption** (if you study).

- Smokin' hot topics, **spicy** discussions.

- Classes are **freshly picked** from the teacher's mind.

- This syllabus is **full of fiber**.

- Take this class and your **acne will vanish overnight**.

- Attending this class (instead of smoking, drinking, and eating fried foods) **may help reduce the risk of heart disease**.

- Every 50 minutes is **packed with energy**.

- **100% original material**, 45% of the time.

- **Premium quality** lessons.

- Tests and quizzes **reduce acid indigestion**.

- **Enriched with** group discussion, games, high expectations, and excellent work.

- When attendance is accompanied with a well-balanced diet, 88% of all class members **experience allergy relief**.

- This assignment will lead to **overnight weight loss**.

- Information is **best if used before**: Exam Date.

- Information **dissolves quickly**, if not reviewed periodically.

Make up some slogans of your own. Just walk down the aisles of your local grocery store and take notes.

I'm going to apologize right now for what I'm about to do—for wasting your time with this next bit, but it's driving my divergent mind crazy and right now I'd rather drive you crazy than me. Grocery. There I said it. A bunch of words ago I mentioned going to the grocery store, and now all that I can think about is the word *grocery*. I attribute a lot of that obsession to the word *grocery* to Lee Chazen, who needed some food because he was hungry after a tennis match. The most common place to buy food at the time (1999) was at a grocery store. Later, we discussed the following about the word *grocery*. Most of the thoughts are his, but I did add things to the conversation like, "I know, uh huh, yep, you're right, and ain't that the truth."

Isn't *grocery* a cool word? It can't really be singular, and yet it is singular. Have you ever purchased one grocery? Hey, I'm going to grab a grocery and I'll be right there. Yes, I just put a grocery in the fridge. Even in the plural it's a weird word. I just went grocery shopping and bought a lot of groceries. Well, how many groceries did you buy? I bought 117 groceries. I have purchased groceries, and I have loaded groceries into the car, and I have brought groceries into the house, and I have put groceries into the cupboards, fridge, and freezer. But then I don't know what happens. I never touch groceries again. Never once have I fixed groceries for breakfast, lunch, or dinner. I have never cut a grocery, opened a grocery, shared a grocery, peeled a grocery, heated a grocery, toasted a grocery, sautéed a grocery, or stir-fried a grocery. But somehow I'm buying lots and lots of groceries every month and they all disappear. Grocery. Groceries.

It all sounded kind of interesting and funny when I was thinking and talking about it, but now that I've written it all down on paper it doesn't seem funny or interesting. Oh well, too late now.

## Lighten Up Rules and Assignments

The assignments (or rules) section of a syllabus is probably not a good place to use much humor. This is one of the few sections that students actually care about, pay attention to, and try to remember—or should, anyway. Hey, I just thought of something. Why not call it a sillybus instead of a syllabus? Ha! I had never thought of that until now. Since I just invented that word, I guess I can also invent the plural: *sillybuses*. Hmm,

I'm going to go back and put that in the title of the chapter! Sounds great. I'll call Webster's!

I generally allow my students to come up with most of our classroom procedures and consequences, so you would not ordinarily find a lot of serious dos and don'ts on my syllabibees. (See Chapter 4.) I do, however, have some nonsensical practices listed with a few sensical (if *nonsensical* is a word, then *sensical* must be a word, too) practices that I want my students to follow. For example:

- During class, please turn off all cell phones, ipods, pagers, beepers, CD players, transistor radios, TVs, stereos, 8-track players, turntables, motorized vehicles, and Walkmans (or is it Walkmen?).

- Do not attempt to operate farm equipment or a Zamboni while reading this syllabus; drowsiness may occur.

- Money-Back Guarantee: Any half-competent student who stays half-awake during this class will benefit from the stuff you learn and be better prepared for stuff that is related to the stuff that we talk about in this class, or your money back (up to $1.99) guaranteed.*

  (*Dr. Hurren reserves the right to determine which students are classified as "half-competent.")

*Humor in School is Serious Business*

I used to put "CLOSED FOR CINCO DE MAYO" on my syllabicycle until a student decided not to attend on May 5th and claimed (correctly) that the syllabus had said class was canceled that day. At least I knew that he had read the syllabus.

Lighten the mood, capture attention, and ensure that they actually read the stuff that you think is important enough to put in writing!

If there are any prerequisites for your classes, you can have some fun with this section by just making up a few, such as these:

- The ability to sit through 50 minutes of commercial-free class time
- Prior knowledge of which end of the pencil writes and which end erases
- Proven ability to count to 20 without using fingers and/or toes
- Mostly regular heartbeat
- Removal of all hammerfingers (more rare than hammertoes, but much more dangerous)

Okay, from here on, you're on your own. You get the idea. Do put creative energy and humor into the forms you give out. Lighten the mood, capture attention, and ensure that they actually read the stuff that you think is important enough to put in writing!

*"I don't work here. I'm a teacher just looking for good ideas to use in my classroom."*

## Chapter Summary

- "Syllabi" is a cool word.

- Syllabi and other class forms can be fun.

- I'm a divergent learner who does not ingest caffeine.

- Steal ideas from multimillion-dollar marketing campaigns and use them on your syllabikes.

## Summary of the Summary

Add humor and sparkle to any written stuff you hand to students or colleagues or send home to parents.

# 8

## Aunt Agatha's Attic, Grandpa's Garage, the Dump, and the Dollar Store

### Tools of the Trade

*"There are uninspired students out there.*
*Quick—to the teacher tool cave!"*

When I write "Tools of the Trade," I mean literal "tools." I literally rip out all of my hair when people use the word *literally* to make a point that doesn't mean *literally* at all. Sports announcers are the biggest culprits, but you can hear the malapropisms, hyperboles, allegories, allusions, metaphors, zeugmas (or whatever they're called) anywhere. How awesome is that? I'm misusing words while talking about my disgust for people misusing words. For example:

- I studied so hard last night that my head literally exploded.

- He literally knocked his block off.

- It's literally raining cats and dogs.

- She literally shot the eyes out of the basket.

- He literally threaded the needle with that pass.

- I literally ran myself into the ground.

- He's literally on fire.

- She literally stuck her foot in her mouth.

- He literally grabbed the bull by the horns and ran with it.

- He literally can't hit the broad side of a barn.

- This book is literally not worth the paper it's printed on.

- This book is literally a piece of garbage.

Anyway, all but two of these examples are literally full of bologna. What I really want to say here is that when I say *literally*, I mean that you should have some delightful, literal tools to use in the classroom.

**Make planned visits to attics, people's garages, the city landfill or random dumpsters, garage sales, and flea markets.**

I have already advocated that you should shop at discount stores to find useful items for spicing up the classroom décor. These are the same places that you can find cheap tools to enhance the learning environment and keep the instruction lively and humorous. They are not the only places, of course.

## The Twenty-first Century Pointer

During the early days of my first year of teaching, I found myself walking around the classroom a lot—usually with a yardstick in hand. It gave my fidgety self something to hold and something handy for pointing at sentences and other information on the board or anywhere else in the classroom. But quickly I began to wonder if there might exist a tool that would be a better pointer. I visited several discount stores and walked the aisles, searching. I came across a cool-looking, flimsy, plastic sword. To my delight, it had a wonderful noise-making feature. It made three different noises, depending on which of three buttons I pushed. One noise was that of two swords clashing together. Another was a high-pitched, fast beeping sound, and the final tone was a low-pitched buzzing sound. The price of the sword was 99 cents, but the value of it in the classroom has been **priceless**!

I use the clashing "ka-ching" sound to point and call on students. Teachers always seem to be looking for ways to get their students to pay attention; well, a sword and the sound of "ka-ching" do that splendidly. With my sword in hand, students' eyes literally follow me wherever I go. (I've almost stepped on many an eyeball in the classroom.) Sometimes I just carry the sword or leave it tucked in my belt and never really use it. But I find that students always pay closer attention when I have an interesting tool or two with me.

When a student answers a question correctly, I raise the sword triumphantly and push the button that causes a high-pitched "beep, beep, beep" sound. And when a student answers incorrectly, I shout, "AAAaaaauuuuggghhhh," clutch my chest and act as if I've been stabbed in the ribs while pushing the buzz button. Any feelings of embarrassment from a wrong answer are quickly absorbed by me and my sword.

I want my students to know what is correct and incorrect, and I want them to know when they have answered correctly and when they have answered incorrectly. However, I don't want them to feel embarrassed or anxious about their answers. The sword and other tools can help erase any embarrassment.

I have another sword thingy that my students call a "light saber." It lights up and makes a "whoop, whoop, whoop" sound when I push a button that I use for correct answers. On days that are more fast-paced or when I need the students to pay extra-close attention, I use both swords, beeping and buzzing and whooping and lights blinking as I run, jump, dance, and point all over the classroom.

## The Must-Have Teacher Tool Belt

The next tools that I'm going to describe are literally my "literal-est" classroom tools. (Okay, the correct grammar here would be "most literal.") When I was building a deck off the back of our house, I couldn't get over how cool I looked with a tool belt strapped around my waist and a hammer hanging from one of the loops. So, while literally cutting and hammering like the wind (and also smacking my thumb a few hundred times), I was also thinking, "How can I incorporate this tool belt and hammer into my classes?" I never really came up with a great idea, but I was determined to wear that tool belt to school and show my students that I am more than a teacher; I can also cut boards, pound nails, and whack my thumb until it turns dark purplish, blackish, and reddish blue. So, I just put it on and wore it to class.

Now might be a good time to explain that I don't do all of these things with a sure knowledge of how they will turn out. I get a little bit "nervousy-ish" feeling and then I just decide to do it and give it my best shot. I have found that whenever

*"I'll take everything!"*

I put energy and excitement into something, the students generally respond. "Generally" in that last sentence means: "ordinarily," "usually," "mostly," or "mainly." This time I was unsure. I had absolutely no plan. I was literally in the dark. But I strapped on my leather tool belt and hammer and started to teach (in the light).

Students had seen me use the sword and a few other tools by then, so they participated quite normally for about ten or fifteen minutes. I began to think, "Good, I look cool and nobody even cares that I'm wearing this tool belt and hammer." But since I hadn't used it or said anything about it, somebody just had to ask, "Hey, Capitán, why are you wearing that goofy-looking tool belt and hammer?"

And at that moment it came to me. The perfect answer literally hit me like a ton of bricks. Please remember that this was a spontaneous answer, but it literally knocked the students' socks off. (Actually, the answer is quite moronic. In fact, I don't even want to share it with you, because 98% of you will read it and think to yourselves, "That's moronic," and the other 2% will say out loud, "That's moronic.") I'm admitting that you're right. What I should've said is, "The reason I'm wearing this tool belt is because I look cool and if you don't pay attention today, I'll whack your thumbs with this hammer." But, what I really said was . . . ugh, I hate to share it with you. Just remember, if I can do and say these half-brained things, so can you. You're going to think it's idiotic, but I said it and students laughed, mostly because it was so dim-witted and unexpected. Okay, enough set-up and justification. And remember, it was spontaneous. Here I go. . . I said, "I'm wearing this tool belt, because today we need extra practice with the tools of grammar."

They stared at me, then a few of them started to giggle, then the giggles infected some others until one student said, "Man, you are weird!"

Then another asked, while still giggling, "Yeah, are you some kind of serial killer or something?"

At that moment all of the laughter stopped and everyone looked at me anxiously. So I pulled out my hammer and said, "Yes, I've already taken care of Snap, Crackle, and Pop and I'm searching for Tony the Tiger right now." Not much laughter to that, but a few giggles and some rolling of the eyes.

Somebody once said something that was somewhat similar to the following quote that is not really a quote from anybody, but the idea is kind of the same: "You can dissect a frog and you can dissect a joke, but they both die in the process" (E. B. White, perhaps). But just in case one of my 43 million readers didn't get that last joke, I will explain it. I heard "cereal" instead of "serial." Now the joke is dead, but the frog is still alive.

I no longer wear the real tool belt, because I now have something even better. I wear a child's fake tool belt and attach plastic fake tools. The kit even came with gloves and a construction helmet. I wear it about two or three times a year, and I do use it to make important points and teach important concepts in a way that helps kids remember.

## Protective Gear and Other Outfits

One day a student who was on the wrestling team came to class with all of his wrestling gear in tow and plopped it all in a pile in one corner of the classroom. Later in the period when students were doing some small-group work, I got curious and started to put on the wrestling gear. Before I regained consciousness, I already had on the headgear, ear guards, kneepads, and elbow pads. As soon as a student noticed, she said, "Capitán, what are you doing now?"

Somewhat embarrassed and surprised, I quickly struck a grappler's pose, or what I perceived to be a grappler's pose, and said in Spanish and in a deep, raspy, wrestler's voice, "We have some very difficult verbs to conjugate today, and if you don't work hard I'm going to put you all in a giant headlock and body slam you and drop-kick you across the room." I left the wrestler's garb on for the whole class period, and the students paid a little more attention that day, but periodically shook their heads in disbelief while looking at me. (Make sure your students all know you are joking when you threaten anything that, even though funny, could sound violent. Use this kind of language cautiously.)

That night, I stopped at several stores to look for some similar gear and eventually settled on purchasing some elbow and kneepads, a cheap biking helmet, and a mouth guard. I didn't use the mouth guard much, but it added a little more mystery to what was going to happen in the classroom that day. I waited a few weeks to try out this get-up with my students. I chose to suit up in my newly purchased padding on the day that I would introduce the subjunctive conjugation to my students, because they generally find this rather difficult to understand.

> When I take time to get creative and act a little nutty for students, they, in return, are more willing to work hard.

This time when a student asked me why I had on all of that stuff, I simply responded, "Things are going to be so rough and tough today that you had better be wearing protection." I know, I know, another simple-minded reply, but students giggled and rolled their eyes, and then they got ready for some fun and challenging work, instead of complaining about having to do hard work or not getting to have a free day. I have found that when I take the time to get creative and act a little nutty for students, they, in return, are more willing to work hard and participate appropriately and energetically in my class.

We often do cooperative activities in my classes. Sometimes I allow my students to choose their own groups; sometimes I assign the groups, and occasionally I use the old hat trick to form groups. Students choose names or numbers out of a hat in order to find their partners or teams. Instead of just a regular old hat, I have a jester's hat. This is an authentic replica of a Middle Ages hat, complete with modern water-resistant polyester microfiber that breathes and liliripes (a real word for the floppy, pointy things and jingle bells). It's just another way to bring fun and humor into the classroom while doing the same stuff and teaching the same material that is needed or required anyway.

## More Attention-Grabbing Tools

The rest of this chapter offers more ideas for tools that can bring creative humor to the classroom, raise interest, and motivate students. This is by no means an exhaustive list. Rather, it is intended to get your brain turning, to inspire a search for your own tools, and to include more humor in ways that best fit your personality (or personalities). Most of these items discussed only cost between 98¢ and $1. They don't have to be used often—just enough to keep you and your students energized, alert, and enthusiastic about the learning process.

**Alligator grabber-picker-upper**—This is sort of an extended-arm device (about 24 inches long) that grabs stuff when you squeeze the handle. Hardware stores sell them for about twenty to thirty dollars, but this one costs only about one dollar at the right store. The actual grabber mechanism is an authentic plastic alligator's head, so its teeth chomp down on whatever you want or need to grab. The more expensive, non-alligator head models are constructed of durable, heavy, metal alloys. The alligator-head version is manufactured using a plastic alloy that is rust-resistant, nonslippery when coated in sticky goo, and comes fully assembled. Another great feature is its ergonomic, contoured handle design. (That is, this is great if your hand is shaped like a wafer-thin crescent.) It can be used to collect papers, grab pencils and pens, pretend to bite students' noses, steal your favorite snack food from students, or simply to chomp loudly at times to remind students to focus. Be careful what you grab. Resist any temptation to behave inappropriately with this (or any other) tool.

**Foam balls**—These are great for keeping students awake and paying attention. You can toss them to the students that are expected to answer questions, write on the board, or ask questions of other students. Students can toss the ball back to the teacher or to another student to participate. They are harmless (unless compressed into a teeny tiny mass and inhaled through the nostrils), and students pay closer attention when there is a chance they'll have to catch or throw a ball.

**Foam shooter doohickey**—Use this on rare occasions. I use it in the same manner as tossing the foam balls, but this tool shoots a ball out of a tube with a puff of air created by the push of a lever. Flight pattern is inconsistent, so it is rather unpredictable as to whom the recipient of the question will be. This makes the event fun, and kids like the cool poof or popping sound when the soft foam ball flies out of the tube.

**Fake bald head**—I have nothing to say about this, except if you have hair, then your students think it's humorous to watch you teach with a bald head. If you are already bald, then get a cheap wig and teach with hair on your head. Act like nothing is different. Then look in a mirror and scream in horror. Students love it. Believe me—this stuff isn't wasted time. It might take up a few minutes, but the humorous focus will cut down on misbehavior, add comfort to the atmosphere, and cut down on kids bugging each other. It will lead to a much more productive day overall.

**Fake microphone**—Teach part of a lesson using a fake microphone that adds an echo to your voice.

**Real microphone**—Sometimes my students have to listen to bits of Spanish on tape and record their answers. I was playing around with one of the recorders and found that by pushing the right combination of buttons I could speak into a microphone and my voice would come out of the speaker. So I strapped the recorder over my shoulder one day and taught using the microphone and the speaker. It made me feel important, and I could make scary breathing noises when I was bored.

*Believe me—this stuff isn't wasted time... It will lead to a much more productive day overall.*

**Giant markers and giant chalk**—Maybe this isn't laugh-out-loud humor, but giant writing utensils are fun, if not funny. Kids will know that whatever you are writing has some importance.

**Weird glasses**—Similar to the bald head or wig, weird eyewear gets and keeps students' attention for a day.

**Helmets**—Teach while wearing a football helmet, baseball helmet, or any other kind of protective headgear.

**Costumes**—I have known teachers who dress up in costume, at times, to match the subject material or current topic that they are teaching. I have heard how much students love this and how well they participate and pay attention on those days. Try this at least a few times a year. Even just a fake nose once in a while will grab their attention.

**Mannequins, dummies, and skeletons**—While searching my mind (as well as the outer recesses and nooks and crannies of the school) for something to help teach a chapter on body parts), I found a real, life-size, artificial skeleton. I put a wig, sunglasses, and a pair of Bermuda shorts on it—and we were ready for class. Different classes gave him different names. Mannequins, dummies, and skeletons can be brought into the classroom to help with lessons on clothing, body parts, etiquette, hygiene, and other appropriate topics.

By the way, if students make fun of the imaginative things that you do in your classroom, let me assure you that they are telling their other teachers how awesome you are and asking them why they aren't more like you. Dare to be different and exciting.

Get to work on your own list of tools. Use them to spark your teaching as well as your students' enthusiasm for learning.

## Chapter Summary

- Bring fun stuff to class.
- Use the fun stuff in class.

## Summary of the Summary

Bring and use fun stuff to capture attention and motivate students.

*"Pay no attention to the gentleman on my left."*

## 9

# Plotting to Fire Up Those Brains

## Lesson Plans with Pizzazz

*"Hmmm . . . a teacher. You're assigned to the lesson plan writing room."*

I have yet to meet a teacher who enjoys making lesson plans. However, just because lesson planning is an arduous task does not mean that we have to punish our students with those same laborious feelings. By actually planning to have some fun at appropriate times during lessons, teachers alleviate feelings of stress and toil among students.

## Get in the Game

Games are probably the most common way to include humor in lesson plans. You can use games to introduce something new, review for tests, or just to play with the information that has been learned. A game integrates reasoning, physical activity, social interaction, emotion,

*Humor in School is Serious Business*

and humor—adding up to more brain engagement with the material you are trying to teach.

**Jeopardy** is a game that works well in most classrooms and for most subject areas. You can adapt it to almost any lesson or group of students, as well as to the technology available. I have played Jeopardy with chalkboards, dry-erase boards, smart boards, and with a computer and projector, as well. When I use the chalkboard or dry-erase board, I have a master list of answers and questions on paper at my "Alex Trebek podium" for the corresponding point values on the board. I also have the theme music from a TV game show playing in the background to add to the excitement and fun. (If you have a computer version—voila! The computer will play the music for you.) A variety of creative and pertinent categories (related to your subject area, of course, with a few wacky categories thrown in) adds to the fun. Over the years, I have honed some rules and guidelines that may help you and your students maintain a little bit of order and keep everyone paying attention throughout the game.

*A game combines reasoning, physical activity, social interaction, emotion, and humor—adding up to more brain engagement with the material you are trying to teach.*

1. To keep arguments to a minimum, tell your students that, for the day, you are Alex (Alexa) Trebek and that you have final say on what is acceptable and unacceptable. Dressing up like him helps. I used to think it was cool to wear a fake moustache for Jeopardy day

when Alex had one, but I think he has shaved it (I'm pretty sure his was real). When Alex Trebek is no longer the host of Jeopardy, or when you want another persona for the host, you'll need to change your name and outfit.

2. Divide the class into three or four equal teams.

3. Use a buzzer system if your school has one. You can probably arrange for students in a shop class or science class to make one. That would be a great learning experience, too. If no buzzer system is available, then rotate turns fairly.

4. Draw straws to determine which team chooses the category and amount first.

5. Rotate turns within each team also. Each individual should be responsible for the buzzer and/or receiving the question individually on a rotation basis.

6. Whoever buzzes in first, or whoever has the turn, can then answer the question by herself or himself for full point value. But if the contestant is wrong, the team loses full point value. However, if the contestant elects to seek help from team members, she or he will gain or lose half the point value. This encourages all team members to pay attention.

7. In order to keep the other teams paying attention, let all participants know that any incorrect answer will return to the question bank and other teams can ask and answer it for full point value.

8. If you have a buzzer system, the last team to answer correctly controls the board. If you do not have a buzzer system, then turns rotate fairly.

9. Have a few hidden Double Jeopardy answers in place, so that teams can risk some points.

10. Have a Final Jeopardy Answer for which teams risk as much as they want. Answers (questions) must be written.

11. Award major points for participation and cooperation, and also give a few bonus points for 1st, 2nd, and 3rd place, with maybe even one point for last place.

**Pictionary** is another great game to use for review of information and ideas. Some of our students are fantastic artists, but they rarely get to show their talents. This is a showcase opportunity for them, and allows them to feel more connected to any class. This game can get quite chaotic and noisy, so I position myself in the middle of the teams to hear their answers, and to let them know when they have gotten too loud.

**Basket Shoot** uses foam balls to shoot baskets for extra points after correct answers are given during review times. I use different lines on the floor for different point values. I've considered putting different baskets at different heights and even awarding extra bonus points if the ball falls through more than one basket.

**Golf Putt**—Putting a golf ball can be used about the same as shooting a foam ball. Just have students putt a golf ball from different distances into a cup or cheap practice hole.

**Paper Football Toss-Kick**—I wonder how many of those little paper, triangular footballs teachers have collected over the past 30 years. You know those things that students flip through a goal post made by their friends' index fingers and thumbs? I tell my students that we will play with them, but only when I say. So as a review, have your students make those little paper, triangular footballs and "kick" field goals for bonus points after questions have been answered correctly. Draw a goal post on the board and students can choose from different lines for different point values. As the teacher it is your job to make the best use of the time that you have, so keep the questions and games moving quickly. That way there will be more time available for more questions and more participation.

## Nutty Reading Material

Be on the lookout for off-the-wall, curious, unusual, and funny stuff that you can share with your students. Keep your mind open for ways to connect that nutty stuff to your content material. Or just use it to motivate students and capture attention. I am thinking of books of blunders, language errors, word mix-ups, and such. For instance, keep copies of some books such as *The 776 Stupidest Things Ever Said* (Petras, 1993), *The 776 Stupidest Things Ever Done* (Petras and Petras, 1996), or *America's Dumbest Criminals* (Butler, 1995). Also add to your collection books or lists of oxymorons, malapropisms, strange idioms, examples of misplaced modifiers, funny mistakes kids make on test answers, and funny mistakes adults make on notes or e-mails or other communications. Share ideas with other teachers. Here are a few examples:

**Misplaced Modifiers**

- *Sue fed the iguana wearing her pajamas.*

- *A green boy's backpack got left in the bleachers.*

- *Lou served a hearty soup to Stu seasoned with paprika.*

- *The teacher saw a snake out the window sitting on her couch drinking her coffee.*

- *Sailing his boat, the shark came very close to Principal Shuman.*

- *Bruised and battered, the bathtub looked good to the football player.*

## Oxymorons

These are phrases that seem contradictory. Students can try to explain the contradictions.

- *act naturally*

- *minor miracle*

- *freezer burn*

- *plastic silverware*

- *silent scream*

- *deafening silence*

- *airline food*

- *good grief*

- *open secret*

- *seriously funny*

- *terribly pleased*

- *cafeteria food*

## Malapropisms

These are situations in which a word is substituted for a similar-sounding word, resulting in a phrase or sentence that is not quite right, and is often hilarious.

- *I had to make altercations in that new dress.*

- *You're a parasite for sore eyes.*

- *She just married the town's most illegible bachelor.*

- *In the Middle Ages, the pheasants paid heavy taxes to the king.*

- *Merchants cursed to India to buy exotic goods.*

- *Quick! Get the fire distinguisher from the corner of the lab!*

- *That test wasn't so hard—it's just a pigment of your imagination.*

- *When the fire broke out, students had to evaporate the lab.*

## Really Dumb Things People Have Said

- *"Hazards are one of the main causes of accidents."*

- *"Things are more like they are now than they ever have been."*

- *"China is a big country, inhabited by many Chinese."*

## Funny, but Real, Headlines

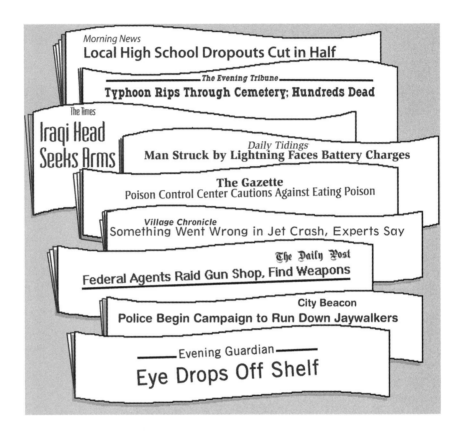

*Morning News*
**Local High School Dropouts Cut in Half**

*The Evening Tribune*
**Typhoon Rips Through Cemetery; Hundreds Dead**

The Times
**Iraqi Head Seeks Arms**

*Daily Tidings*
**Man Struck by Lightning Faces Battery Charges**

**The Gazette**
Poison Control Center Cautions Against Eating Poison

*Village Chronicle*
Something Went Wrong in Jet Crash, Experts Say

The Daily Post
**Federal Agents Raid Gun Shop, Find Weapons**

City Beacon
**Police Begin Campaign to Run Down Jaywalkers**

Evening Guardian
**Eye Drops Off Shelf**

## Mistaken Test Answers

- *When you breath, you inspire. When you don't breath, you expire.*

- *The pistol of a flower is its only protection against insects.*

- *A fossil is an extinct animal. The older it is, the more extinct it is.*

- *The moon is a planet just like Earth, only deader.*

- Nitrogen is not found in Ireland, because it is not found in a free state.

- Three kinds of blood vessels are arteries, vanes, and caterpillars.

- The alimentary canal is located in the northern part of Indiana.

- Before giving a transfusion, find out if the blood is negative or affirmative.

- $H_2O$ is hot water. $CO_2$ is cold water.

- For a nosebleed: put the nose lower than the body until the heart stops.

- Blood flows down one leg and up the other.

## Surprising Excuses Written by Parents (Really!)

- My son is under a doctor's care and should not take P.E. today. Please execute him.

- Chris will not be in school cus he has an acre in his side.

- Please excuse Lisa for being absent. She was sick and I had her shot.

- Please excuse Roland from P.E. for a few days. Yesterday he fell out of a tree and misplaced his hip.

**Puns**

- *It's a drain on our budget to hire a plumber.*

- *Our new P.E. teacher is named Jim Schorts.*

- *That Dracula movie was a pain in the neck.*

- *My surgeon is so funny, she keeps me in stitches!*

- *Our optometrist is Seymour Clearly.*

- *Is a barber who works in a library called a barbarian?*

Have these things ready to use in your class. Kids can examine mix-ups or blunders and figure out why they are wrong. They can rewrite them correctly, translate them into French, turn them into math problems, or apply them to social studies or science lessons. Be inventive—connect such fun stuff to your class material. And once you start the trend, students will be on the lookout for this fun stuff, too!

## Funny Voices, Silly Skits, and Other Lesson Strategies

**Quirky voices**—When you read to your students, use humorous voices for the different characters. This works especially well with the younger students, but it is a great way to attract student attention to any kind of academic information you read aloud. (This is not just for literature.) The first time I did this I wasn't sure how the students would respond, but they roared with laughter. It will serve you well if you practice the voices that you will be using and if you choose fun stories to read or insert wacky ideas into the nonfiction material.

**Skits, plays, songs, and commercials**—All of these help students learn and retain information. I don't want to bore you with any more research, so trust me when I tell you what

Remember the research! Anything that the brain connects with visual images or humor (or both) will be understood better and retained longer.

the research shows: When students create and perform skits, plays, songs, and commercials, they remember more and retain the information longer. Beyond that, these performances give students a chance to show and share their talents. I've often thought that the only students that get labeled "smart" are those with the talents of 1) sitting quietly, and 2) memorizing lots of information while sitting quietly. But what about all of the thousands and millions of students who learn best by doing, interacting, moving, performing, singing, and experiencing? They are often labeled something else—like "underachiever." Let's help all students use, display, and develop their different kinds of intelligences and talents.

Make sure students understand that their creations must be based on content material from the class. My students performed a small section of *Don Quijote de la Mancha* for parents and classmates. Students learned more and retained more about vocabulary, grammar, and literature than from all of my lecture-style lessons combined. (And wow! That doesn't even include the great stuff they learned about planning, organizing, interacting, and cooperating. The learning was vital, critical, useful, and invigorating.)

The same kinds of effective learning took place when my students created their own songs, commercials, and poems as when they created plays and skits. Students had the option

THE SOUNDS OF LEARNING

to film their commercials on location or to perform them live. Some were done as professionally as any I have ever seen on TV.

Most of these risk-taking adventures are done in small groups, but sometimes I assign the work to be solo acts. I always award worthy amounts of points for effort and participation. I've never been a big fan of students doing great big projects for little or no points or just a check mark. I have heard about and witnessed many other teachers from all subject areas that use skits, plays, songs, and commercials with great effectiveness. I have noticed that students pay greater attention to each other's presentations than to a teacher's presentation. I still have some of my students' performances on tape, because some people don't believe how awesome our students can be . . . if we let them.

**Puppets**—I know many teachers (even of middle school students) who use puppets effectively to read, tell stories, and to ask questions. It's fun to see the students give their answers while looking at the puppet. The puppet can make gestures of surprise, sadness, shyness, elation, or even give high-fives to students. Shy or reluctant learners often communicate more easily with a puppet than with a teacher or student audience.

**Cartoons and comic strips**—Make good use of these. Students can write and illustrate their own. All that they need are a few guidelines of topic, possible or necessary vocabulary, length, etc. Or you can use existing strips or cartoons. White out words in the talk balloons so students can fill in what they think should be said. Or give students copies of cartoons with the captions removed. Ask them to add a caption. This can be a writing activity, of course. Or you can require that their caption include one of the week's vocabulary words (used correctly). Students of a foreign language can translate captions. Math students can create math problems relevant to the situation in the comic strip or cartoon. With creativity, you can adapt the use of funny visuals and graphics to **your** subject area. By the way, this book has about 60 cartoons. Think about how you can use them to practice or teach a skill in your class. Remove the captions, if you wish, so that students can add their own.

**Magazine or newspaper articles or pictures**—Have students bring in pictures or news articles to discuss in class—anything they think will spark the interest of classmates and be important or memorable. You can give the guidelines, but allow students to tell how it relates to your subject area. They can do the same kinds of tasks that were suggested for use with cartoons and comic strips.

**Obituaries, tributes, and wills**—This may sound a little morbid, and you wouldn't want to do this activity if there had been a recent tragedy at your school or a death in the family of one of your students. (So use this idea with sensitivity.) But students in my classes have enjoyed writing their own obituaries. (If you don't want to call them obituaries, call them tributes to self.) I find that students are very thoughtful and careful with what they write and how they write it. After we share our future obituaries, I take time to talk with them about not making a mockery of their values and their dreams. I tell them to remember what is important in life and live accordingly. It's also fun to write a will. It's humorous to hear what they choose to leave to whom.

*Your students will learn more and have more fun if you do your best to periodically include some far-out, humorous activities.*

I suddenly feel the need to interject here that I have seen a bunch of fantastic lessons prepared for and given to the "gifted" students, but somehow those lessons never made their way to the average or underachieving students. That saddens me. Please give **all** students the opportunity to be involved in excitement, humor, laughs, and creativity in your classrooms. Okay, back to our regularly-scheduled writing (for me) and reading (for you).

**Kid-created learning material**—I know a great math teacher (Troy Jones) who will remain anonymous, that quickly tired of having his students work math problems straight out of the book. So he asked them to write their own problems and solve those instead. The results have been incredible. Students are working the same types of problems, but they now do them with a sense of urgency and with a real desire to know how to do them correctly. They have been on the baseball field throwing balls and graphing trajectory and speed of the ball. They have determined mathematically how best to throw a ball from different positions on the field with different abilities. They know when to throw an arched trajectory, a line drive, or even when to bounce the ball toward home plate. The unnamed teacher (Troy B. Jones) has borrowed a police radar gun to help his students work problems. The math teacher without identity (Troy Burnell Jones) and his students have helped rugby teams through geometry and calculus classes. They do a ton of other great things in and out of the classroom that I don't understand, because I'm not a mathematicalmatician, but he can write his own book about all of that. Even though Troy Burnell Jones and his lovely wife Cindy (of Saratoga Springs, Utah) will remain nameless to you, I can contact him for further ideas that you mathalytical people might want. Just contact me and I'll contact him for you. I'll include his e-mail address in the chapter summary.

You can also assign students to write funny stuff instead of boring stuff. Maybe not everything that they write will be funny, but it will be challenging to their brains, and will keep them engaged with the learning task.

Not all of the aforementioned ideas are laugh-out-loud, ha-ha funny, but your students will learn more and have more fun if you do your best to periodically include some far-out, humorous activities. I guarantee they will learn more, too. It's a little risky, but teaching is a risky business, so dare to laugh.

## Chapter Summary

- Plan games.

- Play games.

- Be Alex(a) Trebek (or other game show host).

- Read wacky stuff and use it to teach stuff.

- Help students participate in skits, plays, songs, and commercials.

- Be creative.

- Give all students a chance to take part in creating the humor.

- Troy Jones's e-mail is **tjones@alpine.k12.ut.us.**

## Summary of the Summary

That would be awesome if I could come up with some sort of catch phrase here that would sweep the nation. People would quote it in schools and businesses coast to coast, maybe even all over the world. Here it is: "If you plan to fail to play, you can't win." Well, that doesn't make any sense. Maybe: "If you fail to plan to play, then you'll play and fail and plan." No, no, no. "If you fail at playing, you're a failing player." Come on. "If you play for failure, you're not playing with a full deck." "If you play with matches you'll get burned . . . if you start a fire and stick your hand in it." Here it is: "Playing is better than not playing, because, well, because I say so." Ah, whatever—just PLAY!

*Humor in School is Serious Business*

# 10

## LOL and Learn

### Tests and Quizzes with a Twist

*"That's not a nurse. It's my baby's tutor—getting
her ready to excel in kindergarten."*

Goodbye silence! LOL and learn! (If you need a translation,
ask a kid!) The words *humor, fun, amusement, joke,* and
*giggle* are not words that students and teachers ordinarily
associate with taking a test or a quiz. The current intensity and
over-accentuation of testing in the United States is one of our
greatest tragedies. It is catastrophic. At this moment you might
be thinking, "What about Hurricane Katrina?" Okay, you're
right and I'm sort of wrong, so let me restate this. The testing
mania is one of the greatest self-imposed tragedies of all time.
Somehow we brought this upon ourselves and it's here to stay
for a long time. My purpose here is not to rant and rave about
the evils of testing. (That will come in my next book.) My
purpose is to show you how to add humor and sparkle to tests

and quizzes. Nevertheless, I will take a few lines of this chapter to pass along a few of my thoughts on this—in the hope that it will help you be a greater defender of what is good and right.

## The Mild Soapbox Speech About Testing

Okay, I promised not to rant and rave. But I didn't promise not to make a point aggressively. Well, I'll make it mild. (You can skip this section if you don't want to hear my opinions about testing.) Over the past several years, two of my children have brought home excessively-serious letters from school concerning standardized tests and the necessity to score well on them—in KINDERGARTEN. (I'm quite sure that writing in all capital letters means that the writer is shouting. I just shouted.) Both letters stated the names of the tests and the dates that the tests were to be administered. The letters told parents "to practice often with your children, because practice makes perfect." Do you want to know what one-third of the information is that they were practicing? I'll tell you anyway. "Nonsense words." Nonsense words? How about sense words? What about those? I have witnessed children suffer with the "nonsense words" portions of those tests . . . because they know that they are not words! Therefore they score poorly on the test. So if they aren't even words, then why do we call them words? We should call them *qtpxbmkgljds*.

The letters also urged parents "to help students apply their knowledge to different examples used on the test." These are KINDERGARTEN (more shouting) children. The letters ended with, "This test is very important for your kindergarten student. These scores are part of their record and will follow them through their school career." It seems to me that the previous quote from a teacher has some agreement issues, but I'm not going to deal with that any further, right here and now. I just wanted to point it out to you . . . that it's wrong. Maybe that teacher didn't practice enough *qtpxbmkgljds* in kindergarten.

Back to my point: Is it any wonder that our dropout rates are so high? Why do more than one million students drop out of school every year in the United States? Why stay in school for 13 years of misery? I know that I'm asking too many questions here, but I still need to ask two more. Do standardized scores in kindergarten really have any genuine influence on success in life? (I have never come across any study or research that even suggests that could be true. If one exists, I would rather not know about it.) Do **you** have the same abilities, study habits, and tendencies as when you were in kindergarten?

*We need a better, more enjoyable, more balanced, more authentic approach to evaluating our students.*

Our emphasis on testing has made education a relatively closed system. Good memorizers and good test-takers succeed, while all other talents are basically discounted or ignored. Students are tested, retested, and ranked only on their ability to memorize and recall. Jonathan Kozol calls it "drill and kill." We are killing our students' desires to learn and enjoy. And along the way, we are labeling the good memorizers as smart and the not-so-good memorizers as underachievers, students with special needs, and slow learners. In the real world, we are not required to memorize texts, lectures, or long passages. Rather, we are free to search information and friendly advice. We need a better, more enjoyable, more balanced, more authentic approach to evaluating our students.

Please note the following: I am not anti-learn, anti-memorize, anti-math, or anti-science. I just think that we can do a better job helping students enjoy education and get away from the do-or-die attitude with testing. Thanks for reading and caring. Feel free to play some inspirational music in the background. Now back to our regularly scheduled chapter.

## "Fun" in the Same Sentence with "Test"

"Every time I read a funny question, I started paying closer attention and trying harder."

I was about halfway through my first year of teaching middle school Spanish when it first occurred to me to put humorous items on a test. While grading the test, I noticed a jump in scores. At first I did not associate the improvement with the humor. I just assumed that the students found the material from that chapter a little easier, or that for some reason they had all decided to study a little more than usual. As I handed back their tests, I asked what they thought the reason was for the improvement in scores. Immediately a student replied, "Because this test was fun."

Another student echoed the sentiment, "Yeah, every time I read a funny question, I started paying closer attention and trying harder."

Then another said, "I read everything more carefully, because I didn't want to miss anything funny."

I must confess, somewhat guiltily, that when I developed that first test with humorous items, I had no intention of raising their scores or helping them pay closer attention. I was simply a little bored and was trying to entertain myself while creating the test. I also want to make it clear that later that week I went over that test several times to make sure

*Humor in School is Serious Business*

that I had not, somehow, made it easier. I hadn't. My students were right; they had paid closer attention, read questions and directions more carefully, and therefore, scored better on the test. Of course, then my students wanted to know, "Can all of our tests be like that?"

After that experience, I did some investigation and found research to correlate with my rudimentary findings. I will try to bore you for only one short paragraph with this information. Ziv (1976) used a sample of 282 high school students to test the influence of humor on creativity tests. The results of the study (I skipped all of the boring details for you) show that humorous stimuli increase creative thinking during testing. Goodman (1983) found that humor serves to capture students' attention, hold their attention, and free them from distractions, so that they can and will achieve more creative work of a higher quality. Chapman and Crompton (1978) tested the effects of humor on recall. Humorous information facilitated better recall with a mean score of 5.3 compared to 3.4 for the nonhumorous items. This was shown to be significant at the $p < .05$ level (a level that means "wow"). I hope that you appreciate how hard I worked to chop this information down to one short paragraph. Now see how you can put these findings to work—adding humor to your tests.

## Name Switcheroos

In that first experiment of including humor in a test, all that I did was substitute funny names and subjects for ordinary, common, everyday names and subjects. Instead of Jorge and Marta, I used Scooby, Shaggy, and other cartoon characters. Instead of the subjects enjoying, buying, or eating tacos and pizza, they preferred moon pies and cream puffs. Students find it even more interesting when I use faculty and staff names in the tests, and especially when, in the test items, the faculty members prefer SPAM, pickled pigs' feet, gizzards, and calf brains canned in skim milk (all found at your local grocery store). Sometimes I write questions that pair faculty members with movie stars, sports heroes, and other famous and infamous celebrities. Even the principal is fair game. It's such a thrill to see students smiling or hear them giggling during a test. This means that they are paying attention and are not feeling frustrated, distracted, or too tired to finish. Sometimes teachers will come to my room and ask to see one of my tests, because they have heard that their names are in it. This tells me that students are talking about the fun exam. Often, you can safely use students' names in sections of your exams and quizzes. Of course, do this only in ways that are fun while remaining respectful to the individuals. Include your own name. Make fun of yourself.

## On-Camera Stand-up Comedy Quizzes

Sometimes I create tests on video for my students. These mostly consist of me talking to the camera, asking questions of the students. I also make a lot of faces, use different voices, and dress up creatively for different questions. Instead of deleting my mistakes, I just shout "CUT" to the camera, and restate my lines or question. It really doesn't take much longer than writing a quality exam for the class, once I get into character. Students seem to score well on this type of test also. I surmise that the reason for this could be equal parts paying attention and comfort with watching TV. (Research suggests that school-age children watch between 25 and 40 hours of TV and videos every week. They seem to know how to watch TV very well.)

## Not-Your-Ordinary Train Problems

Math problems seem to use a lot of trains and buses (or is it busses?). Hmm, I just looked in the dictionary and it says

*"Laughing rats always test better than grumpy ones."*

that either spelling is allowed. Now I've got to decide which one to use. Maybe I'll choose *buses*, because it will take less time to type than *busses*. Anyway, math problems seem to use a lot of trains and busses, oops, I mean buses, in word problems with distances and speeds. We should use more Porsche Carreras and Ferraris, or maybe a 1967 Mustang convertible, or a 1968 Plymouth Road Runner with a 383 Magnum engine in it. It's also fun to have a math problem that uses the principal's 1974 Gremlin, or 2001 Pontiac Aztec (gotta be the ugliest car ever made), or any teacher's moped with a rocket engine. Or how about some student's skis or skateboard, or the principal on a bungee cord, or a teacher on a zip line?

## Multiple-Choice Surprises

I'm not a big fan of multiple-choice tests. But if you find them useful, please add humor to them. They can be so dull. For instance, if you have three good choices for a possible answer, just add a fourth choice that is comical. If you normally have four possibilities or choices, just add a fifth. Where names are involved, simply add a famous actor, actress, model, sports figure, teacher in the school, city mayor, a cartoon character, or a name that includes a pun (such as a frequently tardy student named Marcus Abbsent, a teacher who drones on and on named Mr. Mel Arcky, or a plumber named Dwayne D. Tubb). Put your own name in there, or use a student's name when appropriate.

Where historical dates are involved, you can add dates in the future, or simply put "my birthday" as a choice.

Where locations are concerned, add fictitious places like Hogwarts and Hollywood (I know, I know, it's a real place, but everything going on there is fake). Use places like Disney World, North Dakota (I don't know, it just seems unlikely), "my house," and Land of the Lost. Or find some of the cities in your country that have strange names. (There really is a Boring, Oregon; a Burnt Corn, Alabama; a Chicken, Alaska; a Wimp, California; a Liars Corner, Ohio; and a Peculiar, Missouri.)

Numbers can even seem humorous. Numbers like bazillion, gazillion, google, lots, tons, and "too many to count" make students smile and feel more relaxed during a difficult test.

## Short-Answer Sass

Adding humor to a short-answer test is simply a matter of scattering a few strategically-placed twisted or ludicrispy questions. Examples will be given later in this chapter.

## The Smart-Aleck Start

Now and then, I like to write some sort of humorous statement at the beginning of an exam or make a humorous announcement before students start. I might, in my most serious voice with my straightest face, clear my throat and say something like, "This is a test. This is only a test. If this were an actual emergency, you would hear sirens, bells, and whistles. Then you would be forced to hurry outside in an orderly fashion, stand in rows without talking to each other, and wait patiently in the freezing cold for the fire department to arrive."

## Students as Humorists

As a partial review and further preparation for an exam, ask students to write questions for the test. When they know that you will use their questions on the actual test, not only will they have fun—they will take the assignment very seriously, I guarantee. Some of my most creative tests have been generated by students. I let each student submit 10 or more questions; then I review them and decide which to include on the test. Because they helped create the test, they feel that they have some insider knowledge. This results in lower stress level and less test anxiety. They even start to look forward to tests!

## Crystal-Clear Directions

Once each year, I like to do a little demonstration about the importance of reading and understanding directions, and the equal importance of asking questions to clarify if anything is unclear. I tell my classes that, too often, students write incorrect answers simply because they were confused about the directions. I ask for a volunteer to give me directions for how to perform a simple task like putting on a jacket and zipping it, or putting on a shoe and tying it. Use your imagination and concentrate, or better yet, think like a young child, and you can have a lot of fun with this. Here are a few examples:

> **Student says:** "Pick up the jacket."

> **You do this:** Toss the jacket in the air or hold it high over your head.

> **Student says:** "Lower it."

> **You do this:** Drop it.

**Student says:** "Put your arm in the sleeve."

**You do this:** Put your arm in through the wrist hole first.

**Student says:** "Turn the jacket around."

**You do this:** Start turning circles while holding the jacket.

**Student says:** "Zip up the jacket."

**You do this:** Zip without connecting the two sides.

As you can tell, you can do almost everything upside down, backwards, or inside out while still following directions. The same is true for the shoe.

**Student says:** "Untie the shoe."

**You do this:** Grab the wrong end of the string and pull, producing a knot.

**Student says:** "Put the shoe on your foot."

**You do this:** Set the shoe on top of your foot.

If the two of you actually succeed in proceeding to the point where the shoe gets on your foot, good luck in getting it tied. Explaining the simple task of tying a shoe is a very difficult task. Giving directions on a test is sometimes complicated, too. This little demonstration encourages your students to ask questions when they are uncertain about your directions. It also

*Tests are stressful enough to begin with. Don't add to the distress by writing murky directions.*

serves to remind you: Tests are stressful enough to begin with. Don't add to the distress by writing murky directions.

## Laughing All the Way to Higher Scores

I alluded to this earlier. But I'll repeat it here: The best thing about humor in tests is that it lowers the stress levels of the test takers, which in turn, raises test scores. I wasn't a strong believer in the "stress lowers test scores" idea until I paid attention to it. I have since read plenty of serious research about this. And the conclusions of many studies affirm that as stress rises during testing, scores drop. I notice the same with my own students. I have had a number of students (what number I don't know, but it's between a few and a lot) who were very, very good at Spanish, but had so much test anxiety that they scored much lower than I expected.

Stress is the state in which a person's valued goals are threatened or lost, or when an individual is unable to create the necessary conditions for obtaining or sustaining his or her goals (Hobfoll, 1998). Although the term *stress* is used liberally, it is not likely that any two individuals claiming to be stressed will be experiencing the same feelings (Edworthy, 2000). Humor reduces stress and improves communication in schools. This increases productivity. Humor also improves morale and makes working conditions more enjoyable. Humor benefits the human body by promoting health and physical healing, reducing stress and anxiety, and increasing hopefulness (Johnson & Indvik, 1990). In times of stress, tragedy, and crisis, humor is a technique used for neutralizing the emotionally-charged area. From the moment that humor is used, the burden is forgotten (Moody, 1978). And importantly, humor improves the level of performance during a stressful task (Crawford, 1994).

## Get Ready, Get Set, Write the Test

One last thought: Let's not get so caught up in testing and test scores that we forget about what is best for the students. Good testing practices take into account the students' best interests. As you read the examples below and as you prepare your own tests, remember that you don't need a lot of humorous items on a test. You choose the number, but just a few will make a positive difference every time. Avoid overkill.

## Sample Test Items

**ENGLISH QUIZ - OCTOBER 3**

*guaranteed non-toxic*

Name: _____

1. The Energizer Bunny has worked longer than (he, him).

2. Count Chocula is older than (I, me).

3. Mr. (insert principal's name) (road, rowed, rode) his boat across the lake, and then got on his tricycle named "The Silver BB" and (road, rowed, rode) it on the gravel (road, rowed, rode).

4. If you stand close to Mr. Grebant and sniff, you will notice a foul (cent, scent, sent).

● **What causes night and day?**

a. The Earth spins on its axis.

b. The Earth moves around the sun.

c. The sun goes around the Earth.

d. E.T. rides his bike to the sun and covers it with his blanket.

- **Circle the pronouns in the following sentence:**

  Kanye West got his name in the news when he insulted Taylor Swift at the 2009 MTV Music Awards Show.

- **What type of magic did the main character practice?**

  a. black magic

  b. white magic

  c. the Magical Mystery Tour

  d. magic to heal animals

- **The boy in the story was traveling by**

  a. pontoon boat

  b. Lamborghini Murciélago

  c. train

  d. magic carpet

  e. bus

- **Which of the following appear to be most responsible for the outbreak of World War I?**

  a. Principal Stevenson and math teacher Torres

  b. Germany and Great Britain

  c. Russia and Austria-Hungary

  d. Germany and Austria-Hungary

  e. Great Britain and France

- **Throughout the war, the most effective, basic new weapon was the**

  a. airplane

  b. machine gun

  c submarine

  d. failure to use underarm deodorant

- **Many people came to the U.S. from Ireland in the 1840s because of**

    a. famine

    b. political revolt

    c. the search for a rainbow and a pot of gold

    d. growth of unions

- **According to Einstein, matter is another form of**

    a. energy

    b. time

    c. mass

    d. light

    e. tapioca pudding

- **All movement is compared with**

    a. a frame of reference

    b. a hemi-powered Plymouth Barracuda

    c. our football team's win-loss record

    d. a tree

- **Our football coach belongs to a flower gardening club. At 49 cents per flower, how many flowers can Coach Hackalarious buy with a $10 bill?**

- **Bob Beamon long jumped 8.90 meters. Basketball coach, Coach Stan Still, cannot jump at all, but he once fell forward 1.62 meters. How many more centimeters did Bob Beamon jump than Coach Stan Still fell?**

- **A manatee can eat 50 pounds of food each day, almost as much as Mr. Gym "Gordo" Teacher. How many pounds of food can a manatee eat in a week?**

*Humor in School is Serious Business*

- ¿A qué hora viene Arnold Schwarzenegger a la casa del Capitán Hurren?

- Are animal crackers an approved dietary supplement for vegetarians?

- When sign makers go on strike, do they write anything on their signs?

- If Wile E. Coyote has enough money to buy all of that Acme stuff, why doesn't he just buy a nice dinner?

- Why are softballs so hard?

- Why does an alarm clock "go off" when it goes on?

- Does it bother you that doctors call what they do "practice"?

- If the majority of all automobile accidents occur within five miles of home, why doesn't everybody move six miles away?

- Why is the person who negotiates with your money called a broker?

- Why do you have to stop at a drive-through bank?

- When Styrofoam is shipped, what packing material is used to surround it?

- Why are apartments always stuck together?

- If cats always land on their feet, and buttered bread always lands butter-side down, what would happen if you Velcroed buttered bread on top of a cat?

## Chapter Summary

- Humor is not usually associated with testing.

- Kindergarten is not as fun as it used to be or should be.

- Nonsense words are . . . just nonsense.

- Testing has gone crazy. It's like "the Blob" out of control.

- Humor on tests leads to higher scores.

- Humor lowers test anxiety (which raises scores).

- Include famous people, infamous people, school personnel, funny words, and funny places on exams.

- Let students write questions for tests.

## Summary of the Summary

Kindergarten students don't need tests, and all other grades need more humor in their tests.

# 11

# Humor Happens to Everyone

## Personal Stories and the Delightful Application Thereof

*"I'm not doing this because it's here. I'm doing this so I have another personal story to share with my students."*

Once, while pushing a shopping buggy down the cereal aisle at the local grocery store, I saw one of my students and his mom approaching with their buggy. The mother did not recognize me, as she was too busy comparing the nutritional values of vitamin-enriched Super Sugar Honey Smackers to those of fortified Triple Sugar-Coated Fruit Loopies. But the boy stopped dead (not literally) in his tracks and dropped his jaw (and the box of chocolate-covered marshmallows he was holding). His eyes widened. I checked behind me to see if maybe Shaquille O'Neal was following me around the store. As I got closer, the student shook his head briefly, blinked hard, and yelped, "Mr. Hurren, what are you doing here?"

> Simple, short, personal stories of humorous and miscellaneous daily events captivate students' attention and teach them that you are human.

I was hungry at the time and unable to conjure up a creative, snappy, or funny response. So I simply replied, "I'm hungry and I heard that they have food here." Not all of your students figure out that you are human and that you require things like food to live. Telling personal stories will help them realize that.

## Put the PS in Your Teaching

This book is saturated (maybe oversaturated, you're thinking) with enchanting personal stories that charm the soul. When you share personal stories (PS) with your students, you get the chance to show them you are a real, live, eating, breathing, and feeling human being. Such stories also offer your students some much-needed relief from stressful events and situations in school. Put simply, the sharing of your own stories helps students enjoy your classes and maybe even like school. Now, if you're reading this book, I assume that you are looking for ways to do just that, because you know that when students enjoy your class, they learn more.

I think I've got something going here with this PS abbreviation. Teachers all over the globe will soon be reminding each other of the importance of using personal stories by whispering "PS" to each other in the halls, at lunch, in faculty meetings, while texting on break and on the freeway, and while staring at 438 different-looking but similar-tasting selections through the stained sneeze guard at the local buffet restaurant.

## Show That You're Human

Hurren once said (in the previous paragraph), "When you

share personal stories (PS) with your students, you get the chance to show them you are a real, live, eating, breathing, and feeling human being." There, now I've cited my own research and quoted myself.

The stories you tell don't have to be magical or full of heroism and super powers. Simple, short, personal stories of humorous and miscellaneous daily events captivate students' attention and teach them that you are human. Oh boy, I almost forgot to tell you. I'm certain that some of you have just been dying to know. Shaquille O'Neal was **not** following me around the grocery store.

Students love food stories. My students especially enjoy hearing about strange foods I've eaten in foreign lands. I did not enjoy every one of these eating experiences, but my students surely love the tales. They like the descriptions of me chewing endlessly on rubbery guatita (cow or goat stomach and intestines) until my gag reflex kicked in and I almost yacked all over a host family in Chile. Fortunately, my cheeks held it all in and I ate a second bite to be polite . . . and almost urped a second time. Each bite was more of the same until my plate was clean.

Other foods I handled more gracefully, if not playfully. My chicken feet soup performed a delightful little dance. I found a way to make the goat's head soup wink at its consumers. My grilled ox tail wagged. I didn't find blood sausage all that disagreeable (other than the thought), but many students love the description. Tongue tacos are quite tasty, and also make for a good story as I describe to my students what it's like to taste something that might be tasting me. Squid are yummy, whether fried or sautéed, as long as you don't look into their eyes. Snails too, can be quite delectable when prepared well. But octopus is much too chewy for me, and the flavor is too strong.

All such stories can be told in twenty seconds to five minutes' time, depending on details given and time allowed for questions. They all have the same effect: You will capture students' attention, show that you are human, and in doing so, enhance your relationship with them.

Here's my students' favorite (by far) personal food story: Responding to a dinner invitation in South America, I was presented with a boiled hoof and shinbone (basically, a cow's leg whacked off at the knee).

My first thought was, "Where has this thing been tromping around?"

My second thought was, "Why are all of these hairs sticking out of the leg?"

My third thought was, "I wonder if anybody here has a loaf of French bread so that I can make a sandwich out of this thing."

My fourth thought was, "Ketchup—I've got to have ketchup—lots of ketchup."

My fifth thought was, "This thing is way too big to shove down the cracks between the leaves of the table like I used to do with spinach when I was seven years old." (Actually, it was ages four through nineteen, but I just decided to average it and then round it off to seven.)

My sixth thought was, "Should I pick up this thing and eat it like a chicken leg?"

My seventh thought was, "Wow, everybody else is almost done with their hooves and shins!"

And my final thought at the dinner table that night was,

"Hmm, tastes like chicken." No, it was actually, "Hmm, tastes like warm, salty, beefy finger jello." Then I threw up and fainted. (JK! If you don't know what that means, ask a kid.)

My point is this: Don't throw up on your host. And don't be afraid to share personal stories with your students. (I'm done using PS. It didn't catch on fast enough.) Sharing your stories draws students closer to you and your subject, and it encourages them to share pieces of their lives with you.

> Use a brief story to defuse a mood or situation that is likely to interfere with the lessons you are about to teach.

## Lower the Anxiety Level

On another noteworthy occasion Hurren (earlier in this chapter), stated that the sharing of personal stories "offers students some much-needed relief from stressful events and stressful situations in school." Personal stories can help everyone relax, forget their woes, and transition to the next serious learning task. Be alert to the times when you can use a brief story to defuse a mood or situation that is likely to interfere with the lessons you are about to teach.

As students were entering my classroom one gloomy winter day after taking one of what seemed like about 183 yearly standardized tests, I noticed that there was an unusually sullen attitude about them. So, after they all came in and got seated, I said, "Let me tell you a little story about our adventurous family walk last night." And then I told the following story:

My wife and I, our two children (we now have five), and our black lab, Noche, all went for a neighborhood walk at about 7:00 p.m. yesterday. About two blocks into the walk, I heard tires squealing and looked up to see a large pick-up truck barreling straight for us as we were crossing an intersection. Susan scooted the children across quickly to the sidewalk, but Noche was paralyzed . . . sniffing a dead frog in the road. I gave a quick jerk on the leash, flicked my foot at him (note that this was **not** a kick, just a mild flick) and shouted, "Come on, Noche!" He looked up and shuffled across just in time to avoid pick-up truck pulverization.

But the driver of the truck didn't see it that way. He brought the truck to a screeching halt and leaped out, pointed his finger at me and shouted, "If I ever see you kick your dog again, I'll personally pound you into the ground and kick you until you're unconscious and then drive over you forwards and backwards, and then you can tell me how it feels to be abused. Now tell me if you're ever going to kick your dog again."

I looked at the guy, looked at Noche, looked at my wife and children, looked at the dead frog, looked back at my wife and children and told them goodbye, and then I said, "Don't worry about it. He's not my dog." The guy wasn't expecting that answer, so he just promised me that we would meet again. My students laughed and forgot all about the crummy standardized test of just a few minutes earlier.

## Share the Pain and Danger

You can do this! You can tell your students about your "accidental" credit card fraud and eventual jail time, or falling off a camel at the zoo, or getting pecked by an ostrich, or getting lost in a cave, or seeing a werewolf, or swerving to miss a duck and running over an alligator, or taking hold of your spouse's hand until she turned to look at you and it wasn't your spouse, or when you sneezed out of your car window but the window was rolled up. I'm certain that you have a brazillion stories like that. Share them with your students (uhhh....maybe **not** about the jail time).

For some odd reason, students seem to enjoy (way, way, way too much) a teacher's personal stories of danger, fear, pain, and trouble. I was walking through a neighborhood in South America one time when machine gunfire broke out. I was scared to death (not literally this time, because I guess I wouldn't be writing this book if that were the case). I didn't know where to turn, where to hide, or even if I should run, duck, jump, hide, crawl, sit, roll over, or play dead. The machine gunfire seemed to be coming from all directions—a terrifying experience for me, but amazingly enjoyable to my students.

For some odd reason, students seem to enjoy (way, way, way too much) a teacher's personal stories of danger, fear, pain, and trouble.

Tell your students about your latest visit to the dentist. They will love it. Explain in great detail what it felt like as the needle pierced your gums and you writhed helplessly in the chair as the drill spun out of control. Your students will roar with laughter. And don't forget the part about the nerve that exploded in your mouth and shot nerve juice out your ear. You will be a smash hit. You'll want to take your act on the road. Think of the awards you will win—Funniest Astute Teacher (FAT), for one.

In March 2000, I got a traffic ticket on the way to school. I delighted my students for the next three and a half weeks by relating the story. I was driving the normal speed limit, but there was a temporary construction speed-limit sign (jammed haphazardly in a bucket of cement on the left side of the road). I failed to notice this sign. When the policeman pulled me over and approached my car window, he asked why I was in such a hurry. I told him that I was a teacher at the high school up the hill, that I wanted to finish grading some papers

*"I liked my science teacher the best,
m'am. Why do you ask?"*

before students came to class, and that I hadn't seen the temporary speed-limit sign on the left side of the road.

He leaned in the window with a big smile and said, "A teacher, huh? My mom is a teacher. What a great thing you teachers do. What do you teach?"

At this point I was thinking, "Yippee, no ticket. I am free, baby. Teaching is the greatest profession in the world." So I said, "I teach Spanish."

He replied quickly with, "Spanish, huh? I always hated Spanish. That was the only class I ever got a D in." And then he wrote me a ticket for double the normal fine, because he said I was speeding in a construction zone. For the next three and a half weeks, my students were in a good mood because of that story.

A few weeks later, I enthralled students again as I detailed my trip to court to contest the traffic violation. The defendant right before me had committed the same wrongdoing as I had, and the judge slapped him with the full double fine. When my name was called and mispronounced, I stepped up and almost abandoned my story. But I didn't, because I believe in telling personal stories.

I told the judge my entire story. I told him how I had been thinking about my students and the day's lessons, so I didn't see the temporary speed-limit sign placed slightly crooked in a bucket of cement on the left side of the road. I stepped closer to show my Exhibit A, a Polaroid photograph of the sign. Looking at the photo he asked, "A teacher huh? What do you teach?"

Just as I was about to blurt out "social studies," I remembered something about perjury and prison. So I nervously tried, "Spanish?"

And the judge said, "You know what I love about you teachers? You always tell the best stories. I could listen to you for hours." Then he leaned his chin in his hands and asked, "So, what do you want me to do?"

I replied, "I want a free pass to drive any speed, anywhere, and any time that I want," and then I gave him a high-five and moonwalked my way out of his court room. Oops, sorry, I was dreaming there. I was so stunned at his question that I just said, "Let me go free, maybe?"

And he did. He said, "Okay," and I walked out, half expecting him to shout, "Stop! What are you, crazy? Pay quadruple the fine, you Spanish teacher you." But he didn't.

Telling personal stories works to your advantage in and out of the classroom.

*Note to reader: You may know a teacher who protests, "I don't want my students to know anything about my life outside of school." Some have said this to me. I say, "Come on. What are you scared of? Students need to make connections with their teachers in order to make connections with the subject matter." So, open up. Spill your guts (again, not literally, and of course, appropriately).*

## Chapter Summary

- Quoting yourself may get you promoted.

- Share personal stories with your students.

- Almost everybody eats food at some point, so food stories relate to a lot of people.

- Don't pop off to big guys driving big pick-up trucks.

- Ask all policemen what classes they liked before you tell them what you teach.

- Tell the truth in a court of law.

## Summary of the Summary

- Avoid the dentist.

- Don't speed.

- Especially don't speed to the dentist's office.

## Shooting from the Hip

### 12

### Spontaneous Hilarity

*"It's a warning to students to expect spontaneous humor inside."*

The use of spontaneous humor is a bit more risky than the other uses of humor that have been discussed to this point. Therefore, I urge you to use caution when attempting it. (You can gather a whole bunch of great synonyms and call this *impulsive* humor, *impromptu* humor, *spur-of-the moment* humor, or whatever other form of unplanned hilarity you want to use as the label.) Anyway, back to my point: Wake up; pay attention; be careful. In the hands of unskilled practitioners, spontaneous humor can be quite explosive, flammable, or even inflammable.

I could stop here and share a long, involved, exciting, and hilarious story about how I learned that *inflammable* is

> Make sure you have some sort of a screen between your brain and your mouth when those impulsive, wacky ideas surface.

not the opposite of *flammable*, but I'll just give you the highlights. I was younger than I am now, but old enough to know better; I'm too embarrassed to actually tell you how old I was. The story went something like this: "Give me that can. I'll show you if it's inflammable or not. I'll bet **I** can get this stuff to burn." KABOOM. AUUUGGGHHH. FIRE. THE SHED. AAAAHHHH. RUN. NO WAIT, STOP, DROP, AND DROOL, or something.

You don't want that kind of situation in your classroom just because you were unskilled in the use of spontaneous humor—or because you didn't know that *inflammable* also means *flammable*. (Somebody in charge of languages and dictionaries needs to change that one, because when a 15-year-old boy picks up a can that says *inflammable* and thinks that it means "impossible to ignite," he takes that as a challenge—a volatile situation when he, also, does not have the necessary thought-processing skills to know or envision that the entire neighborhood could be in danger.) All of this is to say that impromptu humor is a wonderful way to keep students alert and paying attention—and it gives you unlimited opportunities to make learning relevant to specific kids and situations right in your classroom. But **do** make sure you have some sort of a screen between your brain and your mouth when those impulsive, wacky ideas surface.

## Why Use Spontaneous Humor?

There are several reasons why spontaneous humor works so well to get easy laughs. And here they are:

## 1. Surprise

The fact that your students or faculty members have not previously heard the joke or that they were not expecting something funny, means that they will generally laugh more easily. Think about how many times someone has started a story with, "Listen to this; it is so funny," and then you don't find it funny, so you don't laugh, or you use a fake, forced laugh, "Oh, ha ha, yeah, ha ha, funny stuff, ha . . . ha." And then the person is obliged to say, "I guess you had to be there." Correct, you had to be there, because that is when it **was** spontaneous and funny. Surprise students with humor, and they'll laugh without forcing it.

## 2. Connection

When you share humor spontaneously, you connect to your listeners. You share a common experience with them and only them (or so, at least, they think). This is why so many comedians, comediennes, and Canadians start jokes with phrases like, "When I got off the plane in Boston . . ." or Atlanta, or Chicago, or Portland, or Toledo, or Belcher (NY), or Tin Top (TX), or Toad Suck (AR). It connects them with the audience, and it relates to the immediate situation and location.

## 3. Low Expectations

Thanks to all of the boring, less-than-energetic or less-than-positive, ill-spirited, worn-out, calloused teachers in the world, and also thanks to the kindhearted, well-meaning, good teachers who just take themselves way too seriously—expectations for anything funny in the classroom are very low. Sad to say, students don't expect much (or any) humor and fun from their teachers. Thus, they laugh readily when **you** are funny. In truth, many times my comments aren't that funny, or even funny at all (I'm sure you've noticed by now), but students still laugh because the statements are lighthearted—often in serious circumstances. So, maybe I should take a few seconds to say "thank you" to all of the humorless teachers out there

for making me look better than I really am. Ah, it's not worth it. They would never pick up this book and read it anyway. I can hear them now as they glance at my book lying beside the "Best Seller" poster advertising the next great Parry Hotter clone: "Hmph, humor in school. Don't try to tell **me** about humor in school. I've been teaching for 59 years. If students see you smile, it's all over. Instead, I'll buy this new *Larry Dotter and the Boiling Kettle of Fiery Wizardry Wizardness* book."

### 4. Vitality

When you use spontaneous humor, everything you do feels fresh, vital, and new. Students pay attention for longer spans of time because they don't know when you might surprise them with some humor. They train themselves to concentrate, listen, and learn. Remember, nobody wants to be left out of a joke.

## Make Fun of Yourself

While spontaneous humor has its risks—it is a low-risk venture to target yourself with this or any other type of humor. Self-deprecating humor also models a sense of emotional comfort and stability. As teachers, we want to help those students who are easily offended to relax a bit. This is done best in a climate where the teacher can poke fun at himself or herself. Also, this approach contributes to showing your humanity. If you don't take yourself too seriously, students will be able to relate to you more readily.

Whenever I make mistakes in front of my students (about 2,960 times per day), I am quick to make light of my blunder and move on. Comments like the following can help in different situations:

### Self-Deprecating Humor Helps
- *I'm glad to see that my lectures are a cure for your insomnia.*
- *If a four-year-old can operate this thing, why can't I?*
- *I'm an idiot.*
- *I can't believe they gave me a job here.*
- *It kind of makes you wonder if I even have a college degree, doesn't it?*
- *I wish I had finished high school.*
- *I aren't as smart as you think I is.*
- *I guess that's what I get for never using deodorant.*
- *Maybe if I brushed my teeth once in a while, I could think straight.*

When I trip on a student's backpack, chair, or table, I generally exaggerate it and collide into something else. I've banged my shins a few times, but it's always worth the giggle. We laugh together instead of them laughing at me. It's much easier to accept that way.

As you can tell, some of these seemingly-spontaneous comments or actions are almost-planned or prepared. The more you practice spontaneity, the better you get at it.

Not all spontaneous comments are perfect or perfectly appropriate. As I said, it takes practice—along with a good dose of plain old adult wisdom. Between classes, I always step out into the hall to observe and talk to students, as well as to monitor behavior. One time, a couple standing near my door was passionately "making out." Without putting enough thought into my "spontaneitiousness," I said loudly, "Hey,

*"I'm off to practice accidental falls for my classes tomorrow."*

do you mind if I join you?" Students in the area laughed and the happy couple moved on to better make-out territories. Although this got laughs, it was not an appropriate comment for a teacher to make. Again, you get to learn from my mistakes. Keep a leash on your spontaneity.

At a student awards banquet, I was asked at the last moment to take over as presenter for a teacher who had failed to show up. (He was a foreign language teacher—Spanish and French, so the administrator assumed I could handle his presentations appropriately.) The absent teacher infamously wore a T-shirt and jeans every day to teach. So, I started his presentations with, "Mr. Bretang wishes to offer his deepest apologies for not being here in person tonight to honor his students, but his only shirt with a collar is in the wash." Cheers and laughter followed, because nobody was expecting that. It was risky, but kind of funny.

At another awards ceremony, a student was to receive a certificate and pin for perfect attendance. When his name was called, nobody came forward. Not much of a comment

*Humor in School is Serious Business*

was needed—but after a moment of uncomfortable silence, I simply said, "Maybe we jumped the gun on this one." It connected everyone to the experience—hence an easy laugh.

One day, about 20 minutes into a lesson, I got to thinking that I must be the greatest teacher of all time. All students concentrated intensely on my every word. Eyes followed my every move. Then a student finally said, "Uh, you've got a yellow sticky note stuck to the back of your shoulder." I started turning around like a dog trying to find his tail. I spent about 30 seconds just turning and trying to bite the sticky note, students laughing the whole time. The next day, they brought about 493 sticky notes of different sizes and colors to stick all over me.

Now, I need your help. Just today I was stumped, speechless, dumbfounded, nonplussed. With one minute left in class, a student walked up and pulled a scented dryer sheet off of me. I had nothing to say except, "Thank you. Class dismissed." Please send me your creative, spontaneously humorous remarks for that circumstance. It could happen to me again.

Here's a fact about how low the bar really is for expectations of fun in the classroom: The average teacher uses between one-fourth and one-half of a humorous comment per fifty minutes of class time. Don't use a fraction of the joke. Finish the joke. (Okay, to be fair, I guess I should restate the above statement to reinforce the afore-stated statement: "Teachers average between 0.25 and 0.50 humorous comments per fifty minutes of class.")

## Two More Thoughts About S.H.

1. You can throw in unplanned, catch-them-off-guard humor at any time by making silly language "errors."

Go back to Chapter 9 and review the sections titled "Malapropisms," "Misplaced Modifiers," and "Puns." Use a wrong word or an awkward phrasing now and then, and see if students catch it. You can always turn the fun into a mini-lesson, as students ponder what is wrong and how to fix it.

2. As said before (again and again in this chapter), you become a more interesting teacher when you use spontaneous humor. But even better—you become a more **interested** teacher. You become more interested in your students, your surroundings, your subject material, and even your colleagues as you are on the lookout for opportunities to share spontaneous humor.

## Chapter Summary

- Spontaneous humor is risky.

- "Inflammable" means "flammable."

- Spontaneous humor works because it surprises.

- Spontaneous humor works because it connects you with your students.

- Spontaneous humor works because expectations are low.

- Thank the teachers that have set the bar so low, because it makes you look so good.

- Be careful when using spontaneous humor.

- Plan to be spontaneous.

## Summary of the Summary

I'm tired of the word "spontaneous."

## Outrageous Is Contagious

### Over-the-Top Humor

*"If you all pass this biology test, I don't eat you."*

As you become more adept at using spontaneous humor, your humor abilities and comfort will increase to a level where you'll be ready to employ outrageous humor. Like spontaneous humor, outrageous humor can be risky. So be prepared to justify your actions to your fellow colleagues, department chair, vice principal, principal, custodial crew, and a jury of your peers. (Then again, maybe you don't need to justify anything, because you also have the right to remain silent.)

The big advantage of using outrageous humor over spontaneous humor is that outrageous humor is planned. This way you can be more careful with its use. Let me change part of that previous statement and restate it: You usually plan

*Humor in School is Serious Business*

outrageous humor (and you definitely **should** plan it); that way you don't get punched by big, mean people.

## Proceed with Caution

That leads me to my first personal story of this chapter—an example of a situation that taught me to plan my outrageous humor very, very carefully.

Coach Smackilarious, our head football coach, came into my classroom one fine day in February. No invitation, no "Hello" or "Hey" or "How are ya?" Not even a tip of the sombrero or even a glance in my direction. He just came in, stood there for a minute, looked around for three of his players, and then signaled them to go out into the hall with him. Flashing through my mind was the thought, "It's not even football season, what's the big exigency?" (I just now found that word in the thesaurus). The real thought that flashed through my mind was, "Dude, what's up?" Also flashing through my mind like a runaway freight train loaded with plutonium and nitroglycerin was the thought, "Come on, Smackman, your team only won one game all year; show us a little respect until you're at least a .500 team." (That comment doesn't have to be stated here. Even so, I'm leaving it.)

> Plan outrageous humor very, very carefully.

The three students dutifully got up, packed their bags, zipped them loudly, and started to march out of my classroom. Being ever so teensy-weensy, super-slightly infuriated and enraged by this situation, I decided to say (actually I didn't decide anything; it just came shooting out), "We are profoundly absorbed in sagacious concatenation toward the abolishment of ignorance. Please allow us to persevere in the transformation of self and expansion of discernment as we pursue the harvesting of circumspection and enlightenment—Dude." Maybe a little different than that, but you get the gist. He stared at me as his student athletes (or is it athlete students?) lined up at the door with him.

While he stared me, I assumed that he was waiting for a translation from English to English for Dummies, so I said, "Learning stuff going on in here," while moving my arms around in a circular motion to demonstrate "here."

That's when he took two steps toward me and said, "Hurren, one of these days I'm going to mop the floor with your face."

I couldn't back down now, so I said, "You'll find that pretty tough to do, amigo."

A few students were enjoying the collegial exchange and chimed in with, "Oooooooohhhhhhh."

Now, Smackalarious knew that he couldn't walk away from that, but all he had was a predictable, "Why's that?"

Which led to my response of, "Because my face doesn't glide very easily over this synthetic Berber carpet. My delicate skin prefers the feel of 100% natural fibers. And besides, my head doesn't fit very well in the corners." After that we gave each other a high-five and a hug and carried on with our activities, sort of.

## Impersonate Other Professionals

Sometimes I scream—not very often, but sometimes. I'm not in favor of teachers screaming at their students; but screaming **for** them on rare occasions can be invigorating and energizing. You can also use screaming to bring a little humor into the classroom as you imitate what other professionals would be like if they had chosen teaching as a career.

**Drill sergeant**—Start class as a drill sergeant, or announce on a lethargic day that you will be calling on students who are not paying attention as if they were army recruits. "AttenTION. TennHUP. All you PLEEEEBES on your feeeeEEEEET. In your RANKS. Annnnnd HUP, HOO, HEE, FOUR, EVERYBODY OUT THE DOOR. MARCH AROUND the LOCKERS THERE, THEN COME BACK AND SIT IN A CHAIR. HUN, HOO, HEE, FOUR . . . HEE FOUR."

**Baseball umpire**—Tell your students that you have always dreamed about being a major league baseball umpire, so today you will practice making calls throughout the class period. When students seem inattentive, yell, "STEEEERRRRRIIIIIKE ONE," followed by a "STEEEEEERRRRIIIIIIIIKE TWO," etc. And when students expect a called strike, casually give a "Ball one." When a student is not paying attention at all or is purposefully goofing around, scream, "YOU'RRRRRRE OUT!!!" But, please don't send them out of the classroom.

**Baseball announcer**—Or try this—it's even easier. Tell your students that you have auditioned for a minor league baseball announcer's job and you need some preparation, so today you are practicing. Then give play-by-play announcements throughout the class. Instead of, "Drew, answer the next question, please," you say, "Drew steps into the batter's box. He takes a hard SWING, AND IT'S A DRIVE TO DEEP LEFT. THE OUTFIELDER IS GOING BACK BACK BACK BACK BACK. HE'S AT THE WARNING TRACK AND . . . he makes the catch. YOU'RE OUT. Nice try, Drew." Or even better, "IT'S OUTTA HERE!"

*Humor in School is Serious Business*

Other home run possibilities include:

- ADIOS PELOTA

- BONSOIR

- FORGET ABOUT IT

- IT'S GOING, GOING, GOING, GONE

- ELVIS HAS LEFT THE BUILDING

- HE'S GONNA TOUCH 'EM ALL

- HOME RUN, HOME RUN, HOME RUN

**Auctioneer**—An auctioneer-teacher is another role that works. I've only tried this once. It was fun, but more difficult for me. I'm sure that some of you could do it much better. I'd like to see a video of you playing the auctioneer teacher successfully. Send your tapes to: B. Lee Hurren, UNA Box 5119, Florence, AL 35634.

"Who'sgotquestionnumber3whobabywhobabywhobaby whowho'sgonnagivemetheanswerwhobabywhobabywhobaby whooonow?Shawnthinkshe'sgotitShawnthinkshe'sgotit. Let'shearitfromShawngiveitheregiveitheregiveitherenow. SayitsayitsayitSAYIT . . . AND SOLD, TO SHAWN IN ROW TWO WITH THE BLUE SHIRT." Yikes, my fingers are getting laryngitis from all of the screaming. Remember, don't scream too much and always scream **for** the students, not **at** them. And yes, when you do this, you will have a few unwanted visitors check in on you and your students. It adds to the fun, especially if you point at your visitor(s) and say, "Don't make me come after you, too."

**Golf announcer**—You could also be a golf announcer on occasion, especially during the week of one of the major

PGA tournaments. Use a very hushed voice. "Tammy is on the green. She is trying to get a read on this putt. She's sizing this one up and checking every angle and break. I think it's going to go right to left with about 9 inches of break. That's a good putt. It's got a chance. Dead center, wow. That's a nice birdie. Well done, Tammy."

**Others**—Set your imagination to work. There are all kinds of jobs to impersonate, lending spice, energy, and humor to class while keeping students' attention, motivating learning, and strengthening concepts you are trying to teach. The workers you mimic don't have to be people who yell. Just choose professions where things are hopping! Try some of these: short-order cook, waitress hollering orders back to the cook, emergency room worker, air traffic controller, mother of six kids, circus ringleader, boxing match announcer, dance instructor, trainer of tigers, sky diving instructor, and so on.

## Change Your Wardrobe

In Chapter 8, I wrote a little bit about dressing up in costumes to match the subject or topic of the day. But there are also benefits to just showing up wearing something totally unexpected. Your students pay closer attention, and you are a little keener and sharper those days, too. Something I was just thinking about today was those biking shirts. They have those nifty pockets in the lower back for carrying water bottles and energy bars. How cool would that be? In the middle of teaching at 100% capacity, grab a water bottle out of your back shirt pocket, take a few quick sips, squirt your face, and then sling the water bottle across the floor and keep on teaching. That would be awesome. Students would be on the edges of their seats. Add the bike helmet and you're on your way to being Teacher of the Year (TOY). P.S. I don't advise wearing official biking shorts to school unless they are 100%

decent and you really have been biking many miles a day so you fit into them without embarrassing yourself. Oh, and they must, of course, fit the dress code (which they probably don't).

## More Examples of Planned, Outrageous Humor

**Juggle.** I know that not everyone can juggle, but you can learn. I did, and now I can juggle for my students when the occasion calls for it. You can practice with those cheap plastic bags that every store gives to you by the batrillions. Those bags float slowly and they are easy to catch, making them perfect for practicing. (Our local store checker-outers often put just one item in a bag. Who's teaching them to do that? And why do I need a separate bag for each item?) I juggle items representing vocabulary words that they have to spell or translate. If the items are cheap, I toss them out to the class and they can keep them. With food items, we usually eat whatever I was juggling. (Yes, do wash the food before eating it.) If a student answers something incorrectly, I toss it to him or her and it has to be restated or re-answered correctly and tossed back to me. We've broken a couple of raw eggs, but at least I don't juggle them on carpeted floors. If you can't juggle, or you refuse to learn, you can always play toss and catch with the vocabulary items. Whether you juggle or toss, just be careful and wise about what you toss. For example: Don't toss gallon jugs of buttermilk. Or machetes.

*Be careful and wise about what you toss. For example: Don't toss gallon jugs of buttermilk. Or machetes.*

**Eliminate burdens.** One day, my AP students were griping about all of the work that they had to do, which they didn't

*"And I thought a journalism elective was going to be dull."*

feel would even pay off in the end. They were complaining that everything was too difficult, too boring, too time-consuming, wah wah wah. So, I had them write down all of their negative feelings and their fears about the AP exam. Then I collected their lists. They looked at me with great anticipation, assuming that I was going to answer all of their questions and calm their troubled hearts. Instead, I marched everyone outside and had them gather a pile of rocks. Then I laid the papers on the pile of rocks, raised both arms over my head and said, "Repeat after me: We are gathered here today . . . to cast aside our burdens and fears . . . and to remember that we . . . are smart and capable of great things . . . and that we know a lot of stuff . . . and we now commit ourselves to trying harder . . . and doing better . . . and obeying el Capitán." And then I borrowed a lighter from one of my students and lit the papers on fire.

We went back inside and took our places. One student looked at me and said, "That was neat . . . but it didn't help at all." But it did. Everyone felt better, the complaining stopped, and the students were able to continue class with more energy and involvement.

Later that same day, an announcement came over the loud speaker, "Mr. Hurren, please report to the principal's office. Mr. Hurren, please report to the principal's office. To reiterate, Mr. Hurren, principal's office. Hurren, office." The principal wanted to know what I had been doing, so I told him. I emphasized that the students were more eager to study afterwards and that we got a lot more accomplished after the chanting and burning.

A medium-length lecture later, and I was back in class with a better understanding of the federal, state, and local burn codes as well as the penalties for each. Oh yeah, I was also informed of valuable information pertaining to average yearly acreage and square miles of plant life that is destroyed due to careless and thoughtless actions not unlike my own. So learn from my dumb mistakes and involve your administrator as you plan any outrageous humor that involves property or fire. Maybe just putting the lists in a shredder would suffice.

**Write funny recommendations.** Students are always asking me to write recommendations for them to help them get awards, jobs, or scholarships or into clubs, honor society, and other desirable organizations. When a student asks me for a letter of recommendation, I like to write two separate letters. The second letter that I give is solidly written and should be of benefit to him or her getting a job, securing entrance into college, or whatever the goal is. But that is no fun. So, the first letter that I give the requester looks something like the following:

**To Whom It May Concern:**

Marlon asked me to write this here letter of recommendation thing and I'm pretty happy to do it for him because he's a pretty good guy and these are the types of things that I should do if I ever want to get to be Teacher of the Year. I guess that Merlon asked me to write this letter because he thinks a lot of me. But this letter's not supposed to be all about me, know what I mean? So let me say a few things about Merlin. He's allllright. He's one of the smarterest students that I ever done had in my classes. I remember one time in one of my classes that Verlin answered one of them really tough questions that I didn't think he could answer but he did and all I could say was, "Wheuf." Know what I mean? I wish that I could remember the question cuzz you to wood think he was smarter than a lot of other people out there. Believe me, he's smart. And humoristic two. Vermin is funny. He said something funny in class one time that made the students laff and just to show you how funny it was, I laffed also. Now that's funny. Oh yeah Vermit is athaletic. I know that cuzz I think he is on one of our sports teams, unless he quit. I was on a team 2 when I was in school. I could say some other stuff, but I don't know what that wood B. Know what I mean? So anyway, choose Varmit.

SincereLEE,

*Lee*

*P.S. Write back sometime.*

*Humor in School is Serious Business*

**Give unexpected awards.** At our year-end, schoolwide academic awards banquets, I usually like to give my students a little something more than the traditional certificate that ends up on the bottom of a drawer somewhere, never to be seen again. Don't misunderstand, I also give the obligatory certificate so that parents and grandparents can beam with pride for twenty-one seconds as they read the not-quite personalized:

This Certificate of Achievement is presented to _____

for his/her excellent work and/or dedication in _____

class/organization. Congratulations! Date _____

Teacher/Advisor _____ School/Group.

I also give a pin, pen, or compass to offset the paper certificate.

But I can't resist giving something a little more. You know how those awards ceremonies can seem to drag on forever, right? And how hungry you get? Well, I bring my award recipients ice cream on a stick—and I take off the wrapper and hand it to them. That way, they can better enjoy the rest of the ceremony, because they have to eat it or it will melt all over them. It's a little awkward carrying a cooler up to the podium, but always worth it.

# Chapter Summary

- Plan outrageous humor carefully so that you don't get slugged.

- It's a mystery to me why football coaches don't like cross-country coaches.

- Scream like a Banshee for the students, not at them.

- Wear more costumes or outfits to get and hold students' attention.

- Learn to juggle. I did . . . in a tomato-packing shed, and then I got fired, but now it's worth it.

- Even as an adult, I feel like a nine-year-old in the principal's office.

- Certificates get lost.

- Everybody loves ice cream (except for one person in my current department who is lactose intolerant and got mad at me for bringing ice cream to a departmental meeting).

## Summary of the Summary

Plan to scream in a costume while juggling matches, certificates, and ice cream.

*Humor in School is Serious Business*

# 14

## Fixing Hurts and Saving Face —with Mirth

### Making Light of Tough Situations

*"Quick! Say something funny!"*

Making light of unfortunate situations carries considerable risk. So be prudent, use with caution, and practice first by becoming comfortable with low-risk humor in the classroom. But when used on occasion and in the right circumstances, the use of humor to make light of unfortunate situations helps avoid further damage, calms troubled waters, and re-establishes some semblance of control.

## Humor Eases Trauma and Drama

I loved teaching seventh grade reading. I became engrossed in many of the great young adult literary works that I had failed to read or pay attention to when I was a seventh-grader. We read and discussed openly, at times almost acting out parts of the books and our feelings about them.

About 30 minutes into one of these reading classes, a girl in the back row stood up. She looked surprised for a few seconds. Looking back on the situation, I think she was a little bewildered to, all of a sudden, find herself on her feet. But, there she was—up, and she had to go through with her plan now. Her eyes were wide open and she stared right through me. I think she was focusing about six classrooms away. This is what she shrieked,

> YOU DON'T CARE ANYTHING ABOUT US! YOU ACT LIKE YOU CARE, BUT YOU DON'T! YOU THINK YOU'RE SO GREAT! WELL YOU'RE NOT. I'M SICK AND TIRED OF BEING IN THIS CLASS. I WISH I WAS NEVER IN HERE! I'M GETTING OUT OF THIS CLASS AND IF I HAD MY WAY, I'D NEVER COME BACK TO THIS SCHOOL! YOU DON'T EVEN CARE ABOUT US AT ALL!

She was breathing so hard that I thought she was going to hyperventilate. One of the thoughts to flash through my mind was, "Send her to the office." But for what? I scream sometimes, too. Another thought was that maybe we should review classroom decorum, but that didn't seem the appropriate response either.

This girl fully expected to be sent to the office. With her X-ray vision, she could probably already see her reserved seat there. But I focused on her near-hyperventilation state and said rather calmly, "Oh good, I see we have a volunteer standing at the back of the room. Clarissa, take question number three, please." We were not even going over any questions at the time. Now she was as stunned as I was. A few students snickered at my comment. Clarissa waited to be sent to the office, but it didn't happen.

*Humor in School is Serious Business*

Since she was still standing, I said with extreme tranquility in my voice, "Thank you, Clarissa, for your thoughts, but if you don't have anything else to share with the rest of the class you may sit down now if you like." I heard a few more giggles. She sat down, but I don't think she blinked for the rest of the period.

When class was over, I asked her to stay and talk to me. I asked what was going on. I reminded her that I do care about my students and that I often let them decide what we read, how we discuss, and what other activities we do in a semester. She agreed, but didn't say much.

A few days later, her parents came to see me. I was prepared to apologize if they felt that I had offended or belittled their daughter. I was also prepared to defend my philosophy and methods of teaching and classroom management. But they wanted to thank me for the way I had handled the whole situation. I asked how they knew.

They said, "We read our daughter's diary at least once a week. Did you know that she has a crush on you?"

I blushed, looked at my feet, and started drawing circles with my toes. All I could say was, "Garsh." No, no, no. I said, "Well, middle schoolers can get a little confused."

Then her parents said, "We'll take care of it." She was an excellent student the rest of the year and the following year in my Spanish II class, as well.

## Humor Defuses Disaster

You may or may not want to follow my example in this next story. But, for this particular circumstance and the two students involved, humor defused a volatile situation, and we all got back to work.

Seemingly out of nowhere (or maybe I wasn't very "with it" on that particular day), Jason and Eric were out of their respective seats and began a stare down. They stared at each other while biting lower lips (each his own) and trying hard not to blink. I had never had anything close to a fight in my classroom. I simply did not know what to do. So, I stared. Then the chest bumping started. I think they inherited that trait from their closest intelligent relative, the rooster, or the bighorn sheep. It is something to watch. I don't know what to call that something, but it is something. The middle school boy (girls never do this) places his arms slightly behind his back and to the side. He then unlocks his double-jointed mandible, juts out his chin approximately 11 inches, and approaches his arch nemesis with his head back, concave chest out (if that's possible). Then they simply bump chests.

At this point, I shouted, "LADIES AND GENTLEMEN. IN THIS CORNER WE HAVE JOLTIN' JASON JONES TAKING ON ERIC ERASE-YOUR-FACE TIMMONS." I was prepared to keep announcing, but at that point they both looked at me and shook their heads and Jason started laughing.

Then Eric said, "You are so weird, man."

To which I replied, "Yeah, you two are really normal." The class laughed together, and the two boys actually agreed that I was the weirdest of all. After class, I had a good talk with them, and they were put in charge of room clean-up for a week. I reminded them that, had punches been thrown, the discipline would've assuredly been handled by the administration.

## Humor Eases Embarrassment

I used to love chalkboards. There was something exciting, electrifying, and fantastic about writing on an old-fashioned chalkboard with chalk—the sound, the chalk sparks, the dust on your hands, clothes, and in your lungs—the coughing, gagging, and resulting emphysema. Okay, maybe it wasn't as romantic as I remember it, but I kind of miss chalk.

However, there is a way to make a very embarrassing sound with chalk. It almost always occurs by accident. In fact, it is very difficult to perform on command. Somehow when the chalk is angled downward just perfectly (72 degrees) and exactly the right amount of pressure is exerted (5.3 psi) on a down stroke at the perfect speed (2.1 feet per second), well, you get a sound that makes your students think that you ate way too many frijoles the night before.

The first time that it happened to me I didn't think much of it. But then, I'm not a seventh-grader. After my students finished laughing and I finished rolling my eyes to the back of my brain, I explained that it was the chalk and not any noises of flatulence. Then I attempted to get us all back to work. But

*"And in this corner we have two young bucks in a stare-down, displaying their prowess to impress the rest of the herd."*

*Humor in School is Serious Business*

every time I thought we were back on track, a student felt the need to imitate the sound, "Pbbbbt," which was quickly followed by laughter and more, "Pbbbbt." Some made the sound with their mouths, others with their mouths and arms; still others used hands and armpits while flapping one elbow like a chicken. That day we did not accomplish much.

The next time that the chalk toot happened, I was ready. It was over a year later, but I was ready. I jumped and spun around to face my students with a surprised look on my face. Then I simply said, "Excuse me," and went on. They laughed, but because I beat them to the laughs and made fun of myself, they didn't feel the need to go around the room taking turns blowing, spitting, and pumping out "Pbbbbt" sounds. We had some fun over it, but this time we were able to carry on with our learning.

And you see that humor, even subtle, can cut down on distractions—just as it can defuse and smooth out lots of other tough, volatile, or unfortunate situations.

## Chapter Summary

- Don't send students to the office unless absolutely necessary.

- Don't advocate student fighting.

- Chalk has its hazards.

- Don't always use me as an example of what to do.

- Be careful.

## Summary of the Summary

Be very careful with chalk.

# Comedy Begets Camaraderie

## Using Humor with Your Colleagues

*"I regret that I have but one body to give to classroom humor."*

The title of this chapter **should** be "Comedy Begets Camaraderie (Usually)." But since the actual title is true in most cases, I'll stick with it. Maybe I should start by telling you about my favorite funny experience with a colleague. (In truth, I have not completed this experience, but one day I will. I'm just sure that it will be hilarious (if you're there, of course); but it could also be a little dangerous. Possible side effects are scratches, cuts, bruises, abrasions, lacerations, fractures, compound fractures, loss of vision, lingering back pain, concussion, hyper-extended something, pulled muscles, turf toe, broken bones, sprains, strains, torn rotator cuff, plantar fasciitis, and maybe death. Even with those risks, I still gave it a try, sort of. I just ran into a little roadblock.

## Going All Out to Cheer a Colleague

Here's the idea: You remove one of your ceiling tiles and crawl up into the ceiling space. Then crawl over to the space above a colleague's classroom. This alone is very dangerous, because you cannot crawl on the tiles. They will not support your weight. I'm not calling you overweight; they just won't hold more than about 15 pounds. You have to find and reach water pipes and support beams in the dark—while avoiding electrical wires, phone wires, possum families, and opossum families. (Now that I think about it, a flashlight or headlamp is an idea—though not one I thought about when I started on this venture.) Anyway, once you arrive at a spot directly over the favorite (or least favorite) colleague's room, you wait for just the right moment. Then you crash down into the classroom full of students. Just look around and say, "Excuse me, is this room 304? Hmm. I must have taken a wrong turn." And then walk out.

Wouldn't that be great? You would be a legend at that school. That might even become your nickname: "Legend." Of course, you also might be the main attraction at a funeral a few days later.

What a stunt—right? I honestly explored the feasibility of pulling it off. I got the idea when I was crawling around above my classroom in order to rewire my clock and phone system to accommodate the talking teddy bear phone. I did try to make my way over to some other rooms, but our walls extended above the level of the ceiling.

An easier option is to sneak into the classroom after school, spend the night above the ceiling, and crash down the next morning. I intended to try it, but wasn't sure I could keep my balance on the water pipes all night.

I think the real reason that I never followed through with this scheme was that I was afraid of miscalculating my drop zone, or of the possibility that a student might be standing or sitting in the drop zone, or of spending the rest of my life in a severely injured state. (Losing my job might be another undesirable consequence.)

Teaching is the richest source of comedy in the world (other than politics, of course).

Other than crashing through ceilings, humor with colleagues is quite safe. The same basic rule that applies to sharing humor with students is in effect here: Know your audience and act accordingly. Humor should not be intended to demoralize, but to invigorate, cheer, and build enthusiasm. Sharing humor together as a faculty carries over to positive feelings of fun and excitement in classrooms with students. The more teachers enjoy working with each other, the more teachers enjoy their classroom teaching experiences as well.

## A New Day—A New Laugh

One of the best things about teaching is that every day is different. A teacher never truly knows what will happen on any given day. So, look at that as a benefit; plan for novelty and surprise. Set up little e-mail (or text) dialogues with colleagues that document the fun, funny, and bizarre. When you find a funny headline, wacky story, appropriate joke, or great pun, be sure to share it. (Be wise about what you text and e-mail.)

A wholesome dose of humor in any workplace is an indication of a flourishing and invigorating environment. When people enjoy each other, they enjoy the work they perform, and when they enjoy their work, they work harder and better. Teaching is the richest source of comedy in the world (other than politics, of course). Have fun with teaching.

> Your purpose is not to make fun of, embarrass, or slander members of your school community, but to have fun with them.

Share the delightful aspects and humorous incidents. The challenges of your job will look less like burdens for you and fellow staff members. And when there are burdens, you'll have an already-established rapport that will help you lighten them for each other. Humor is, without doubt, an easy way to build collaboration and more connection.

## Announcements, Altered

The following are real announcements and e-mails that I received from administrators and office personnel at different schools where I taught. These are representative of messages that we all receive, which sometimes seem to be a waste of time and energy—especially when they come as class interruptions. I became a little frustrated early in my teaching career by the number of announcements, phone calls, e-mails, and delivered messages for which we had to interrupt the learning process. So I started creating humorous responses or additions to these messages, and then shared them with colleagues. Sometimes I did this through e-mail. Sometimes the student body officers would allow me to deliver my humorous messages during assemblies. And at other times, I would stealthily sneak into the announcement room and seize the microphone from the student announcer. The e-mail messages are fairly safe (although, these days, even **they** can be less than private). The other two methods might be considered a little more high risk. Please remember that you need to know your audience, and that your purpose is not to make fun of, embarrass, or slander members of your school community, but to have fun with them. The original announcements are in italics, with my comments in and around them.

*Humor in School is Serious Business*

- *Please put teacher-of-the-month nominations in the suggestion box before Friday's assembly.* That way Mr. Hurren will be sure to not win again.

- Unbelievably, these next two announcements were made for a full week at one of my schools, and they were right next to each other. *Reminder to students: The couch and chair by the office are for guests only.* Next announcement. *Students and staff: Please be reminded that guests are not allowed on campus.*

- *Due to liability concerns, students are not allowed on the athletic fields at any time during the day.* I say we sell the couch and chair, and then buy some insurance so that we can use our fields. Or, let's put the furniture outside and we can play football on it.

- After what seemed like an endless list of announcements for club meetings, I said, "There will be a meeting club meeting today at lunch to decide how many meetings can be listed in the meeting section of the announcements."

- *The Debate Team will meet this week.* Debaters are still debating when and where to hold their meetings.

- *The Gun Club is seeking spare arms donations.* They are also accepting legs and other appendages.

- A Special Note to Faculty: *Please let the office know if you want your December paycheck mailed home*, so that you can afford to buy your family a delicious holiday sparrow for dinner.

- *The library will be accepting cans of food* so that librarians everywhere can enjoy a nice dinner. Canned hams are preferred.

- *The County Sheriff's Department will be conducting canine drug searches on campus for the remainder of the year.* All dogs found on campus with drugs will be incarcerated.

- For all students who are sick and tired of teachers telling them what to do, *there will be an army recruiter on campus tomorrow at lunch.*

## Tricks and Tummy-Tickling Tidbits

Get in the habit (with the agreement of other staff members) of playing fun little tricks on each other. A few times I snuck (sneaked? sneakered? snucked?) into other teachers' classrooms in between classes and put my head down on a desk. After the class started, I snored loudly. When I was discovered, I acted startled, wiped some saliva off my face, apologized, and asked for directions back to my classroom. A couple of times, I kept my head down on the desk and made comments like, "We've already done this. This is boring. Why do we have to do this?" (Though not the most productive way to spend my planning period, it brought a little laughter into other teachers' classrooms.) When you do things like this, just make sure that you choose a teacher who welcomes the fun and the small disruption to the class.

As teachers, we are blessed to receive dozens of humorous statements each year that students write on homework assignments, essays, and tests. When you share these, they will brighten a colleague's mood. Pass them on with care, however. Don't give students' names, and don't share a statement with the purpose of belittling someone.

*"Stand back, students! This looks like
a job for Stress-Reliever Man!"*

Below is just a small sample of some gems that I have received:

- *I'm going to be an English teacher because I talk real good and I can write.*

- *Our results is that we finished our assignment.*

- *In this science experiment, I filled the balloons up with water and threw them. Green goes the farthest.*

- *Integration is more than just desecration.*

- *This is just demoral.*

- *I think that segregation is when they disintegrated blacks and whites.*

- *There are 1.7 million students in U.S. schools and 1.2 million of them are in home-school.*

- *The jest of the meeting dealt with money.*

- *That tied the score at 4 to 3.*

> *Make a commitment to keep humor alive for each other.*

- *That makes so much of no sense that I don't even want to explain it.*

- *Schools need more brakes.*

- *A right angle is the opposite of a wrong angle.*

- *We do not automatically know everything from day one and then go learn more.*

- *One more reason that it wasn't as important back then is because it wasn't as important back then as it is today.*

Professional athletes give us memorable quotes on a regular basis. Here are just a few to share with colleagues:

- *I take my hand off to him.*

- *Maybe now I can just fade into Bolivian.*

- *To accuse me of that is ludicrisp.*

## Plan for Staff Humor

Watch for ways to add humorous sparks to the school days of your colleagues. Here are a few things to keep on your list. Get other staff members in on the act by making a commitment to keep the humor alive for each other.

**Share fun stuff with colleagues.** When you do this, you lighten their spirit and build a sense of shared mission. Tidbits such as the lists above can also provide that other teacher or coach with some fun stuff to use with their students. (See more ideas in Chapter 9 under "Nutty Reading Material.") For instance, they can ask students to analyze each of the statements. Students can draw conclusions as to what is wrong with the statements, make corrections, and research to find accurate information. (For example, students can pursue these

*Humor in School is Serious Business*

questions: "What is wrong with the 'I take my hand off to him' statement?" or "What is the more frequently used expression, what does it mean, and where did it originate?") Keep your eyes open for things that pertain to a particular subject area. Colleagues will be pleased that you are intentionally watching for things to help them add fun to the material they teach.

**Add comedy to staff meetings.** Start every staff or committee meeting with a good joke, funny reading, or cartoon. Take turns being responsible to bring something that will brighten up the end of a tiring day.

**Dedicate a hall bulletin board to humor.** Keep a bulletin board for jokes and cartoons that poke fun at teachers and school. Make sure this is in a place where everyone can enjoy it—including students. They need to know that teachers can have fun.

**Lighten up assemblies and school events.** Make a point of getting teachers and other staff members involved in school-wide assemblies, parties, and other events. Rally the troops to have a teacher skit or staff talent number. Kids love to see the adults act crazy. But that's not the biggest benefit. Brainstorming and planning a skit, getting costumes together, rehearsing, and performing together—that process does wonders for faculty-staff camaraderie and for stress release. Of course, these are the moments the students will remember, and they'll have a lot more respect for their teachers. And I guarantee that when there's an assembly coming up, student attendance rates will soar and tardies will plummet. No one will want to miss such comedy!

**Switch places for fun.** Join with another colleague and plan to surprise students with funny switches. Show up in one another's classrooms now and then with an outrageous claim, tantalizing mystery, hilarious costume, shockingly stupendous bit of wisdom, or embarrassing story about the fellow teacher. You can even plan a funny interruption that turns into a math lesson, social studies research challenge, science CSI investigation, or language arts task such as practicing interview skills.

Humor lurks in the halls, classrooms, fields, and other corners of any school. All you have to do is find it. Watch for ways to spread lightheartedness to overstressed co-workers. Do this in a spirit of helpfulness. You will find yourself liking your colleagues better. And if you can approach this without doing obnoxious stuff, they may like you better, too.

## Chapter Summary

- Make sure you have plenty of insurance before dropping through the ceiling.

- Share humor with colleagues.

- Look for humor in daily occurrences.

- Teaching is fun; share the fun.

- School is fun, and at times funny; share the humor.

- Students are funny; share their funny comments and antics with other teachers (but do so anonymously and respectfully).

- Sharing humor with other teachers makes school a better place.

## Summary of the Summary

Find humor and share it appropriately and often with fellow teachers.

# 16

## Smiles in the Field, on the Track, in the Pool, and Onstage

### Using Humor in Coaching

*"Okay, Coach, we ran till we were sick. Is this sick enough?"*

Many sports are inherently fun. That's why we call them games. I coach distance runners on the cross-country team and we have a saying that goes like this: "Cross-country: The only true sport. Everything else is just a game." However, most cross-country teams are quite small, because it's not a game, and therefore it may not be perceived as fun. Cross-country has nothing to throw, catch, kick, hit, swing, punch, or smash, so I have to work a little harder to help distance runners have fun at practices (or else I'll end up running by myself every day). Because there is a certain level of conditioning required with every sport, and because conditioning or running seems to be the least desirable part of many practices, I now share with you a few ideas for helping athletes through this process. (This can be applied to swimming and other conditioning activities. If you coach thumb-wrestling or drama, you'll have to adapt these ideas to your own practice activities.)

## There's Fun in the Run

Before I launch into my ideas for helping you help your athletes enjoy running, I must tell you that I feel quite strongly about encouraging people to enjoy running. I feel quite strongly about encouraging people to enjoy running. There I told you. Running is an activity in which people can casually participate throughout their lives, for fitness or to relieve stress, competitively or noncompetitively, alone or in groups or on teams, on trails or on roads or on grass, in neighborhoods or in rural or suburban areas, when it's cold or hot, in rain or snow, at high altitude or on the beach, anywhere and anytime. It's relatively cheap. There is very little equipment needed. It's really good for health. So why don't more people stay fit through running? I think it is, in part, because so many coaches have taken the fun out of running. Think about it. Children love to run. Tag, hide-and-go-seek, and most of their made-up, outdoor activities are just running games. Children run after butterflies, ducks, squirrels, leaves, armadillos, and almost anything else that moves.

And then some little league coach (of any sport) gets mad at his or her team members and punishes them by making them run. She or he screams something like one of the following at them:

"Now run until it hurts."

"Yeah, well maybe you won't lose next time. Get back on the line."

"Run until you can't run anymore and then run some more."

"I don't care how bad it hurts, keep running."

"Run until you puke."

"You're going to run until you remember to never drop the ball again!"

"Get up and run. And stop clutching your chest."

All of the above are real quotes—and I guarantee you, they are from coaches who don't run (or otherwise condition) with their athletes.

My brother coaches several soccer teams of different ages. He called me and said, "My players hate to run. How can I make them like it?"

**So, Coach—stop yelling and start running!**

I answered, "Run with them."

Before I could explain my response to him, he countered with, "No way. You must be crazy. I hate running. I've always hated running. I hate running with a passion. I hate running so much that . . ."

I cut him off, "Okay, okay, I've got it. You don't like running. And that's a big part of why your players don't like running, either. Make it fun for them. And the best way to make it fun for them is to run with them."

We can't always play the sport with our athletes, because of age, size, liability, and anger-management issues. You may not be able to do those backward flips in gymnastics. And the cheerleaders on your squad will **not** want to toss you in the air, I assure you. But in any sport, we coaches can run with them to help them get into good condition. Athletes of all ages love to have their coaches run with them. Suddenly, running becomes fun, mostly because they see you hurting as much or more than they are. They run just as hard as before, maybe even harder. They accomplish just as much as before, maybe even more. But now they hate it less—and maybe even enjoy it.

When you run with them, you also build team unity. Athletes are more disciplined, have a greater desire to work

*"I never cared much for dodge ball until
the teacher started joining us."*

harder, and perform better for a coach who is willing to work as hard as they do. So what if you don't beat all of them (or any of them)? In addition to working harder, your athletes will appreciate and respect you more when you train **with** them instead of yelling at them. So, Coach—stop yelling. Start running. I've got other ideas, but you will be amazed by the difference this one change makes in your team dynamics and the efforts displayed.

Not every running exercise has to be just a line-up-and-run-till-you-toss-your-cookies experience. Here are some varieties:

**Relays are great ways to involve everyone in running for fun or for competition.** The relays can be as long or as short as you want them to be, and you can have as many on a team as you want. Each runner can run as many legs of the relay as you want. The rest interval is simply the time that the partner(s) spend running their sections. Athletes can choose numbers from a hat for their partners, or you can purposefully group faster team members with those who are slower. You can also let them select their own teams at times. They run even harder when they know that team members are relying on them. Put yourself on a relay team, too, or form one with all coaches.

*Humor in School is Serious Business*

**Make up or create an obstacle course and have athletes race through it.** They can run around and through goal posts, goals, fences, dugouts, bases, fields, benches, bleachers, sheds, fountains, sprinklers, lawn mowers, light poles, creeks, and nets. You can also have them hurdle over benches or crawl under them. Use swings, slides, jungle gyms, and other playground equipment as part of the course. Every time we run obstacle courses, my runners say things like, "Man, I thought that was going to be fun and easy. It was fun, but it was one of the hardest workouts we have ever had," or "Man, I'm beat. That was tough." But we also laugh and retell stories of running, diving, jumping, sliding, climbing, etc. In the end, it is still a great workout with a lot of fun, laughs, and stories.

**You can also combine the previous two ideas.** (Use relay teams on an obstacle course.)

**Invent your own games.** Have everyone take off his or her shoes and put them all in a pile. Then on a command, they must all find their own shoes, put them on, and run to a certain point and back. Or they have to put on the first shoes that they grab and run. Or have a scavenger hunt that requires all participants to run as they search for clues or items.

**Try handicap runs.** This simply means giving your slower runners a chance to get a head start and see if they can hold off the faster runners. Release them in as many groups as you want, or even individually.

**Do calisthenics in between runs.** After each burst of speed, athletes do a set of sit-ups, push-ups, or other repetitions. This is a great way to increase core strength, as well as develop greater cardiovascular ability.

**Involve water and getting wet, weather permitting.** Water relays develop endurance, speed, coordination, and strength.

Divide into teams. Place large buckets of water at one end of the course and an equal number of empty buckets at the other end of the course. Every bucket should be numbered and have a "twin" matching number at the opposite end. Each runner is given two small paper cups. Each team is assigned a bucket number. The object is to run back and forth—dipping, filling, running without spilling, and filling the empty bucket. You can go until the water reaches a certain mark on the previously-empty bucket, or go for a predetermined amount of time and then measure to determine a winner. Winners receive a prize of a free sports drink or getting doused with the water that is left in the buckets. Turn on as many sprinklers as possible and create a relay course that utilizes every sprinkler on campus.

Join in on the hard work. Humor helps a lot, but its effects triple when you participate in the work you are asking them to do.

Send me other ideas, and I'll use some of them in the second edition of this book—if there ever is one.

As an aside here: I know too many teachers who use the harsh coaching model and punish students with long reading or laborious writing assignments. When little children first learn to read and write, they love it. They read everything possible. They read every sign they see from the family minivan, every sign they see on the road, every cereal box, billboard, and everything everywhere—until someone punishes them with a reading assignment. They create stories, write names, invent words, write letters, and even start a seven-part mini-series—until someone punishes them with a writing assignment. Then they lose interest, or even want to avoid these things. If a coach uses the very skill desired for the sport as a punishment, athletes will grow to hate the activity that is supposed to bring them joy and fulfillment. Don't take the fun away. Create fun. Oh, and remember, participate with them.

## Fun in the Hard Work

All sports are hard work. Any coach (even if it is for something that is not a typical sport—something like debate or drama) has the job of trying to motivate students to work hard, and at the same time, to grow and develop as persons. Every strategy and every bit of advice given earlier in this book is applicable to the coaching setting. Remember that humor relaxes students, relieves the stress they bring with them to practice and competitions, lightens up the mood and helps them drop their worries, helps them think creatively, relieves pain, grabs their attention, and shapes examples they will remember. Laughter makes people feel better. Use it! All these uses of humor will serve you well as you prepare your athletes for competition or just for enjoyment of the sport. And once more I'll say this: Join in on the hard work. Humor helps a lot, but its effects triple when you participate in the work you are asking them to do.

## Fun in the Relationships

Teams or clubs of any sort are dependent on relationships. As a coach, you want to build a respectful, warm, working relationship with your athletes. And in order for any team to work well, there must also be amiable, respectful relationships between the team members. I hope you read all the previous chapters. Because if you did, you will be able to apply the ideas therein toward building the relationships needed for successful coaching—ideas such as these: Humor, used appropriately, eases tensions between students. Humor builds connections between human beings. Humor can defuse volatile situations and give relief when things seem disastrous (maybe things like losing a game or having the best player injured or a referee treating your team unfairly). Humor gives you a way to let athletes know you like them and care about them.

Whether you coach cheerleading, football, wrestling, debate, lacrosse, cricket spitting, or extreme basket weaving—skip the "Run till I tell you to stop, and, by the way, you'd better be throwing up or you have not worked hard enough." Instead, get them laughing.

## Chapter Summary

- Distance running is the only true sport.

- Run with your athletes.

- My brother's name is Hank and he hates running.

- Use relays.

- Make and use obstacle courses.

- Have relay races on obstacle courses.

- Run with your athletes.

- Invent running games and tell me about them.

- Use water.

- Run with your athletes.

- Use humor to relate to your athletes.

- Don't yell and belittle. Laugh instead.

- Participate with your athletes.

## Summary of the Summary

Throwing up is never fun, but the workout can be fun.

# 17

## Hail to the Chief Clown!

### Humor for Principals and Other School Leaders

*"I'm sorry, Mrs. Samuels, but we have a zero-tolerance policy for any student bringing a sharp wit to school."*

I have read plenty of boring research over the past 20 years, but only one piece of work surpasses my own dissertation on the Spectrum of Dullness. (My dissertation, *The Effects of Principals' Humor on Teachers' Job Satisfaction*, contains almost 200 pages of the most powerful and productive anti-insomnia medication known to man . . . and my wife would like to testify of its equally potent effect on women.) I'm tempted to reveal the author and work that I consider even more boring than I and mine, but at this point in my career I am incapable of sustaining a lengthy lawsuit. I'll try not to bore you too terribly throughout this chapter, but I offer no guarantees. If you find yourself blinking heavily and nodding considerably, just stick your face in a bucket of ice for three seconds and then continue reading. Or fluff your favorite pillow and begin counting sheep with the big dogs until the cows come home (while wearing the cat's pajamas, of course).

## Tough Problem, Happy Solution

[In at least one state], the dropout rate for teachers is higher than the dropout rate for students.

In the United States, approximately 35% of all public school teachers seriously consider leaving the profession. I would be okay with that statistic if those 35% were the mean, crummy teachers, but my experiences lead me to believe that it is usually the enthusiastic, hardworking teachers that quit or consider quitting. A newspaper in the state of Alabama recently reported that the dropout rate for teachers is higher than the dropout rate for students. The reason for such a high rate of teacher attrition is simple: They are dissatisfied with their jobs. But why are they dissatisfied? At the top of teachers' lists of complaints is "difficulties with the administration" (Engelking, 1986; Miller, 1991; Tishler & Ernest, 1989).

*Note to principals: Do not get mad at me! Hold your fire! This information does not mean that you are rotten, no-good, crooked, lousy, dishonest, vile, scurrilous, filthy, stinking, untrustworthy leaders. It just means that we now need to answer the question: "What can administrators do to increase teachers' job satisfaction?"*

Answer: Use more humor. According to Ziegler and Boardman (1986), humor just may be the necessary ingredient for enhancing organizational goals while promoting personal fulfillment. Therefore, **do** consider humor (seriously) as a

*Humor in School is Serious Business*

constructive force within an organization. Humor has the potential to be a very useful tool for school principals. My dissertation measures and demonstrates that principals who share more humor in the workplace have teachers with significantly higher rates of job satisfaction. I feel that the positive effect of an administrator using humor in school is so powerful that it is beyond measure. Before I performed that study, nobody had ever measured the value of principals' humor in schools. I'm not bragging and I'm not trying to say that I deserve a Pulitzer or a Nobel Prize, or even a noble prize, Olympic gold medal, or dinner invitation to the White House—or, for that matter, a dinner invitation to **your** house. I'm just saying that what I did was one of the greatest feats ever accomplished in the history of dissertationalismness. But it's still fairly boring.

One of the problems with performing a serious study about humor is that nobody wants to take it seriously. Several members of my committee told me that I could not do the study. When I asked why, I was told 1) because nothing like it has ever been done before, and 2) because it sounds kind of frivolous. It took some work, but I was able to convince them that it could be done and that I could treat it seriously (hence the boringness). As I mentioned earlier, I don't want to bore you to sleep, but I want all principals and future principals to know a little about how this study was performed so that they and their subordinate staffs may comprehend the power of humor in their positions. I will make every effort to keep it brief and not abusive, bromidic, or boringfied.

Of the principalship, Barth said, "Humor is sorely lacking in this profession."

> Schools are funny places with a lot of funny things happening in them. Principals should make better use of humor.

My own visits, observations, and studies, combined with two decades of work in schools, plus reading, writing, and teaching—all helped determine that during an average day, a principal engages in several hundred interactions, very few of which include humor (Barth, 1990). Of the principalship, Barth (1990, p. 515) said, "Humor is sorely lacking in this profession." He says that schools are funny places with a lot of funny things happening in them, and that principals should make better use of humor. Barth (1990, p. 515) also stated, "People learn and grow and survive through humor. We should make an effort to elicit and cultivate it, rather than ignore, thwart, or merely tolerate it." Teachers' sense of satisfaction, as well as a school's accomplishments, may depend on the leader's sense of humor.

## Giggles, Guffaws, and Goodwill

I studied school climate and determined that principals have significant influence on the climate of a school—more influence than anyone else. A healthy school climate is often found in a school where a principal appreciates and shares humor. Pierson and Bredeson (1993) revealed that administrative use of humor helps create and improve school climate by forming an environment of connectedness between teachers and administrators. Research suggests that humor can promote flexibility, facilitate communication between principals and teachers, provide alternative perspectives, and promote a feeling of goodwill—all factors that affect school climate (Ziegler, Boardman, & Thomas, 1985).

A middle school principal and assistant principal in Virginia decided to change the culture of their school by incorporating

*"You know, Principal Smith, making them laugh*
*is not part of your job description."*

more humor into activities and meetings. They altered faculty meetings to begin with fun games; they organized parties during the most stressful times of the school year; they added cartoons and jokes to announcements, bulletins, and the school newspaper; they hung humorous photographs in halls and the faculty lounge. The staff responded positively, meetings were more fun, and more students and faculty were involved in positive conversations. The school's teacher evaluations showed more teachers incorporating humor into their classroom instruction—and more students paying attention because of it. The simple incorporation of humor by the school's leaders had a dramatic effect for good on teachers and students at that school (Lane, 1993).

A leader who does not share a sense of humor with his or her workers may become a source of much stress to those workers. Studies have shown that educational administrators, especially school principals, are sources of stress among teachers (Blase, Dedrick, & Strathe, 1986). Humor releases tension that otherwise might exist between administration and staff. A principal's use of humor improves morale, reduces stress, and improves communication in schools—which is likely to make working conditions more enjoyable and improve productivity.

## Successful Leadership Is No Joke

To many, a sense of humor is a necessary attribute of a good leader. Executives from 18 of the United States' largest school systems were asked what it takes to be a successful leader (Wilson, 1991). There was unanimous agreement on the top answer: that, in order to be successful, a school executive must possess qualities that go beyond what a school board seeks. A sense of humor ranked third on the list of the necessary attributes. Without humor, according to Wilson, a leader will experience difficulties and ultimately fail. Marlowe (1995) determined that more work is accomplished **because** of laughter than in spite of it, while leadership without humor will result in fewer overall accomplishments. The clear fact is this: A sense of humor is an indispensable tool of an effective educational leader.

In an attempt to learn what makes outstanding school leaders successful, representatives of the U.S. Department of Education held a meeting with educators who are well-known for their leadership and school improvement efforts (Nadeau & Leighton, 1996). A questionnaire was distributed at the meeting. Respondents placed a sense of humor at the top of the list for effective leadership. Humor enhances the quality of communication and reduces the gap between super-ordinate and subordinate, as well as creating a sense of belonging for all members of an organization.

Teachers' job satisfaction is important to the future of schooling and the teaching profession. Therefore, principals have an obligation to administer in styles that produce

> I believe that the positive effect of an administrator using humor in school is so powerful that it is beyond measure.

satisfaction. Humor is a strategy that principals need in order to raise teachers' job satisfaction. Humor must be used as a stratagem to conduct business in schools.

My not-yet-award-winning-study-but-maybe-in-the-future-if-enough-of-you-vote-for-me was designed to investigate the frequency of humor use by school principals and its relationship to teachers' job satisfaction. Because over 90% of human beings rate their own sense of humor as "above normal," I determined that the teachers, rather than the principals themselves, would best evaluate the frequency of their principals' use of humor. A total of 650 surveys were mailed to public school teachers. A 72% return rate demonstrates high interest from teachers in the topic. (It's interesting to note that middle school teachers had a 95% return rate. I'm not sure what it means, but it's interesting.)

I won't further bore you with details of the methods of the study, but there were several categories for determining frequency of principals' use of humor in different situations. At this point (the point of loud snoring), it is probably sufficient to let you know that there are significant positive relationships between the frequency of principals' use of humor and teachers' job satisfaction. The connection is positively significant! Principals who share more humor in school have teachers who feel more satisfied with their jobs.

A curious point of observation here is this: Principals enjoy a greater advantage than teachers when sharing humor, because the bar has been set even lower for them than for teachers—the expectation for principals lurking at the bottom of the ocean (whichever ocean is deepest). Faculty, staff, and students laugh easily when principals make even the slightest attempt to share humor.

## Strategies to Start the Humor Growing

Below is a list of suggestions that principals may find useful as they encourage and include the use of humor in their schools:

- Seek a sense of humor.

- Laugh with teachers.

- Laugh with students.

- Analyze what makes you laugh and experience more of it.

- Analyze what makes your colleagues laugh and include more of it.

- Analyze what makes the students laugh and use more of it.

- Memorize a few one-liners, jokes, and stories.

- When hiring personnel, identify the use of humor as an important characteristic of a good staff member.

- Take part in assemblies, games, and activities. (Stick your neck out!)

- Infuse humor into daily announcements.

- Give high-fives and humorous comments to students in the halls.

- Seek from **other** principals examples of how **they** have used humor.

- Include humor and jokes at awards banquets and ceremonies.

- Include humor, even if memorized, in faculty meetings.

> *Humor enhances the quality of communication and reduces the gap between super-ordinate and subordinate.*

- Review the information in Chapter 3 about how humor relieves stress. Then use that to minimize your own stress.

- Review the information in Chapter 7 about adding humor to student forms. Then use the ideas to add humor (appropriately) to the forms you distribute.

- Review the discussion of "tools of the trade" in Chapter 8. Come up with a few of your own tools and costumes. Use one when you really need to capture attention and make a point.

- Reread all the ideas in Chapters 11, 12, 13, and 14 about using personal stories, spontaneous or outrageous humor, and humor to fix hurts or save face. Then apply these to your daily meetings, issues, and confrontations. (Reserve the outrageous humor for very select occasions.)

- Share with your staff the research on the benefits of humor. Some will take the laughter more seriously if they see its importance in print or hear it from the experts. (This is just in case of the slight possibility—highly unlikely, of course—that you might have a staff member who is resistant to believing anything **you** say.)

- And maybe the most important idea of all: Encourage teachers to share humor in their classrooms with their students and with their colleagues.

*Note to reader: If you want even more sleep-inducing material to read on this topic, please contact me at **blhurren@ una.edu** or come visit me in person to read my own unread copy of my dissertation.*

Leaders, the above list should get you started, but the goal is to adjust your mind and habits so that such ideas flow naturally. Use these as models and inspiration to invent your own strategies for making humor in your school serious business (sort of).

## Chapter Summary

- A lot of teachers consider quitting.

- I wish that the crummy teachers would quit.

- My dissertation is boring.

- I have not won any awards.

- Principals have significant influence at schools and should share more humor.

## Summary of the Summary

Principals who use more humor have teachers who are more satisfied with their jobs and more excited about their teaching, and therefore, have students who are more enthusiastic about learning!

# 18

## Blinking Yellow Lights and the Hippocratic Oath

Humor Guidelines and Cautions

*"Your dog is suffering from an overdose of insulting jokes."*

Congratulations! You have made it a long way. I must admit that I never thought that you would faithfully hang in there all the way to Chapter 18. It's not that I doubt your reading ability; it's just that I never expected anyone would read more than twenty or thirty of my words, much less over 46,000 of them. Now that you have come this far, you might as well read the whole book. I'll do my best to keep these last few chapters short, if you will agree to keep reading and finish the book. Deal? Good. Now I can tell you that this chapter probably won't be very funny. What? (I heard you whisper, "None of the other chapters were funny either.") Well, anyway, the reason for this chapter not being funny is because it isn't humorous. Furthermore, it's downright serious.

*Please do not use humor carelessly.*

It is imperative that I mention a few guidelines (almost rules) about the use of humor. They don't need much, if any, explanation. But they really must be included, because—if we get sloppy with the use of humor, it is easy to offend students, co-workers, and others. Please do not use humor carelessly.

1. Avoid making jokes about nationality, religion, sexuality, sexual orientation, body configurations or issues, ethnicity, disabilities, gender issues, or death.

2. Avoid insults.

3. Avoid laughing at people or poking fun at people. It is better and safer to laugh together at situations or at yourself.

4. Be careful with sarcasm; use it **very** sparingly.

5. When you make a mistake and possibly hurt someone's feelings, apologize quickly.

**The end.** (I told you this chapter would be short. If you want a chapter summary, just reread the chapter!)

Okay, okay, for those of you who are only reading the chapter summaries, I will include one here, too. (You are probably one of those people who saw the movie or read the *Cliff Notes* of those books you were supposed to read in middle school, high school, college, and grad school—right?)

## Chapter Summary

Be careful when using humor, because it can hurt people's feelings or cause problems for people (you bonehead).

## Summary of the Summary

Don't say hurtful things.

*Humor in School is Serious Business*

# 19

## Laughter on Purpose

Conclusion

*"Nothing different EVER happens here."*

There is one more chapter after this, so make sure that you read it. I promised my publisher that I would have 20 chapters. Plus, I do have a few more important ideas that I wasn't sure where to include; so I'll just make up a chapter title and put them at the end.

For weeks, I've been pondering what to say in this concluding chapter. I have nothing. So, maybe it's a good thing that this is not the last chapter. You are probably wondering what kind of an author would have nothing to say in conclusion. You might be thinking, "Well, I could write a conclusion to this book even if this nut can't." Aha! This is a brilliant tactic on my part! I say that I don't have anything to say. And right away, that gets you thinking about what I should say. If you have read this book and taken it seriously, you **could** write the conclusion. So do it. Write a sentence or two that wraps up the message of the book:

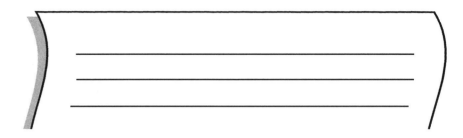

Then, in the right setting, try the same trick with your students. Pretend that you have nothing to say as a concluding wrap-up to a lesson, unit, or key idea. (Maybe you won't be pretending.) Act clueless or exhausted or confused—and pass the job on to them. They'll have to review, synthesize, and summarize. This is just the kind of stuff you want kids to do!

And now, since you've done such a good job of doing my job—let's turn to your job. What will you do with the ideas, nutty stories, research, and strategies you have read in this book? Think hard about it. Then, set at least five goals for yourself for using humor in your school or classroom. Write them inside the back cover of this book. Better yet, post them in a prominent place (such as your bathroom mirror) so you can check up on yourself periodically. If you're nervous about doing such a big job by yourself, enlist your students or a colleague in the goal setting and work on this together. However you choose to do it, make sure you take seriously the benefits and joys of adding humor to your school—and start laughing more often with your students!

## Chapter Summary

Humor works. Get busy and use it. (Anything longer would be longer than the chapter.)

## Summary of the Summary

H. W. (Anything longer would be longer than the summary.)

# 20

## The Serious Sport of Comedy

This book has been mostly about sharing humor in school and having fun with students. However, I am keenly aware that teaching is a tough, gritty, arduous, difficult, strenuous, exhausting, unyielding, intense, and sometimes brutal job. In order to survive, a teacher must be tenacious, strong, rugged, durable, resilient, Herculean—and humorous. All of the above adjectives are used abundantly in descriptions of sports and athletes. Since teaching and teachers have so much in common with sports and athletes, I propose that we begin treating our profession more like professional sports and ourselves more like professional athletes (or their coaches and trainers). Allow me to explain.

When you teach a good lesson with passion, humor, and excitement, students should be encouraged to applaud. Step it up a notch—and there should be yelling! fist pumps! and standing ovations! Give your students those long, air-filled

> There's no reason why all that anticipation, cheering, and chanting should be saved for the bleachers, huddles, dugouts, or grandstands.

clapper things that fans wave behind the backboard when opponents shoot free throws in basketball, and encourage their use in your classes to applaud success, good ideas, and clever products. Insert high-fives into speeches or presentations (given by you or students) when an emphatic point is made. Sign autographs periodically. Allow appropriate displays of disappointment in the crowd (such as when you double the homework).

The idea is to borrow the energy, team spirit, and celebration that are the best aspects of sports—and channel them into active participation in learning. There's no reason why all that anticipation, cheering, and chanting should be saved for the bleachers, huddles, dugouts, or the grandstands.

## Start Your Own Traditions

The world of sports has wonderful traditions and rituals. Borrow and adapt many of these to boost morale, esteem, camaraderie, and unity. As a school or as an individual teacher, you can periodically select a sport and include some of its practices in ways that are fun and appropriate for your situation, class, and personality. Here are just a few examples:

**Football**—Before class starts, have students line up and run through a tunnel of some sort (even if it's just your doorway). As they run through, they have to slap a sign above the door that says something like one of the following: *Elevate your minds, All it takes is all you've got, Learning is everything,* or *Passion!* Occasionally huddle-up and call some plays. "All right, everybody in here. It's fourth and long. We're going for it. Now listen, here's what we're gonna do . . . Is everybody with me? On three, ready, BREAK."

*Humor in School is Serious Business*

*"In a very bold move, Williams is now all in. Does he know the*
*Civil War History answer, or is he bluffing?"*

**Baseball**—Bring a baseball and mitts to class. Invite a student to throw out a ceremonial first pitch. (Choose someone who has accomplished something in any arena—not just your class—or for any other worthy reason.) Play the classic organ music that gets played at baseball games and then have everybody shout, "CHARGE!" or "PLAY BALL!" And, how about a little chatter from the infield? "C'monNowLet'sGoYouGotThis OneUseThe#2PencilNowAttawayAttawayToGo!"

**Basketball**—Do the Globetrotter weave with your students. Distribute things to them with behind-the-back passes or under your leg (as long as you're not wearing a dress). On this day, students can shoot their trash without penalty. Give points when they make their shots. Throw some powder or chalk dust in the air like LeBron James. Use a twenty-four second shot clock for answering questions.

**Tennis**—Have a towel that you periodically use to dry your hands and face, and then toss the towel aside. Bring your racket and some balls to tap to students as you call on them. Assign a ball boy and a ball girl to occasionally stand at attention, raise a ball high over their heads and wait for your signal to toss it to you. Every ten minutes or so, sit in a chair, take a sip of water, dry off, and switch sides of the room to teach. Points on this day are awarded as *Love, 15, 30, 40, Deuce,* and *Game*.

**Golf**—Have a leader board that you can change. Put students' names on it and a few teachers' names, if you dare. Talk softly. Every once in a while, remove your golf hat and yell something undetectable into it. Assign a student caddie to give you advice on your teaching for the day. Confer with him or her at times to decide whether or not to go with the workbook assignment or a different activity.

## Any Sport Will Do

Don't limit this idea to the most traditional school sports. Learn the rituals and rules of cricket, lacrosse, chess, water polo, ping-pong, curling, and other sports. Include actions generic to all sports. Make up cheers and chants together. Start a Hall of Fame with a mini-induction ceremony. Retire people's numbers. When a great teacher retires, retire her or his classroom number or phone extension and hang up the number on a wall for all to see.

Most importantly, laugh with your students, have fun with your students, and share humor with your students. After all, **humor in school is serious business** (sort of).

## Chapter Summary

Teaching is tough, but exhilarating. Do all that you can to cheer and have fun.

## Summary of the Summary

Have fun! And be sure to write and tell me about all the fun and exciting things that you are doing in the classroom with your students. Oh yeah, and HAVE FUN!

## Chapter 1

McDermott, P. & Rothenberg, J. (2000). Why urban parents resist involvement in their children's elementary education. *The Qualitative Report, 5,* 3–4. Retrieved August 05, 2009, from **http://www.nova.edu/ssss/QR/QR5-3/mcdermott.html**.

## Chapter 3

Adair, F. A., & Siegel, L. (1984). *Improving performance through the use of humor* (Report No. CG 017 783). New Orleans, LA: Southeastern Psychological Association. (ERIC Document Reproduction Service No. ED 250 584).

Anderman, E. M., Belzer, S., & Smith, J. (1991). *Teacher commitment and job satisfaction: The role of school culture and principal leadership.* Chicago, IL: American Educational Research Association. (ERIC Document Reproduction Service No. ED 375 497).

Berk, L. S., Tan, S. A., Fry, W. F., Napier, B. J., Lee, J. W., Hubbard, R. W., Lewis, J. E., & Eby, W. C. (1989). Neuroendocrine and stress hormone changes during mirthful laughter. *The American Journal of the Medical Sciences*, 298, 390–396.

Caine, R. M., and Caine, G. (1991). *Making connections, teaching and the human brain.* Alexandria, VA: ASCD.

Caine, R. M., Caine, G., McClintic, C. L., Klimek, K. J. (2004) 12 Brain/Mind Learning Principles in Action: *The fieldbook for making connections, teaching, and the human brain.* Thousand Oaks, CA: Corwin Press.

Chapman, A. J. (1983). Humor and laughter in social interaction and some implications for humor research. In P. E. McGhee, & J. H. Goldstein (Eds.), *Handbook of research, volume I, basic issues* (pp. 135–157). New York: Springer-Verlag.

Chapman, A. J., & Crompton, P. (1978). Humorous presentations of material and presentations of humorous material: A review of the humor and memory literature and two experimental studies. In M. M. Gruneberg, P. E. Morris, & R. N. Sykes (Eds.), *Practical aspects of memory* (pp. 84–92). London: Academic Press.

Chapman, A. J., & Foot, H. C. (Eds.). (1996). *Humor and laughter: Theory, research, and applications.* New Brunswick, NJ: Transaction.

Csikszentmihalyi, M., & McCormack, J. (1986). The influence of teachers. *Phi Delta Kappan, 67*, 415–419.

Edworthy, A. (2000). *Managing stress.* Buckingham, Great Britain: Open University Press.

Ellet, C. D., & Walberg, H. J. (1979). Principals' competency, environment, and outcomes. In H. J. Walberg (Ed.), *Educational environments and effects* (pp. 140–164). Berkeley, CA: McCutchan.

Fine, G. A. (1983). Sociological approaches to the study of humor. In P. E. McGhee, & J. H. Goldstein (Eds.), *Handbook of humor research, volume I, basic issues* (pp. 159–181). New York: Springer-Verlag.

Firestone, W. A., & Rosenblum, S. (1988). Building commitment in urban high schools. *Educational Evaluation and Policy Analysis, 10*, 285–299.

Frankl, V. E. (1963). *Man's search for meaning: An introduction to logotherapy.* Boston: Beacon Press.

Fry, W. F., & Salameh, W. A. (Eds.). (1987). *Handbook of humor and psychotherapy: Advances in the clinical use of humor.* Sarasota, FL: Professional Resource Exchange.

Goodman, J. (1983). How to get more smileage out of your life: Making sense of humor, then serving it. In P. E. McGhee, & J. H. Goldstein (Eds.), *Handbook of humor research, volume II, applied studies* (pp. 1–21). New York: Springer-Verlag.

Hurren, B. L. (2006). The effects of principals' humor on teachers' job satisfaction. *Educational Studies, 32*, 373–385.

LaFave, L., Haddad, J., & Maesen, W. A. (1996). Superiority, enhanced self-esteem, and perceived incongruity humor theory. In A. J. Chapman, & H. C. Foot (Eds.), *Humor and laughter: Theory, research, and applications* (pp. 63–91). New Brunswick, NJ: Transaction.

Malone, P. B. (1980). Humor: A double-edged tool for today's managers? *Academy of Management Review, 5*, 357–360.

Moody, R. A. (1978). *Laugh after laugh.* Jacksonville, FL: Headwaters Press.

Riley, D. M., & Furedy, J. J. (1985). Psychological and physiological systems. In S. R. Burchfield (Ed.), *Stress: Psychological and physiological interactions* (pp. 3–15). New York: Hemisphere.

Rosenholtz, S. J. (1989). Teachers' workplace: *The social organization of schools.* White Plains, NY: Longman.

Wilson, S., & Cameron, R. (1994). *What do student teachers perceive as effective teaching?* (Report No. SP 035 485). New South Wales, Australia: Australian Teacher Education Association. (ERIC Document Reproduction Service No. ED 375 108).

Ziv, A. (1976). Facilitating effects of humor on creativity. *Journal of Educational Psychology, 68*, 318–322.

## Chapter 10

Chapman, A. J., & Crompton, P. (1978). Humorous presentations of material and presentations of humorous material: A review of the humor and memory literature and two experimental studies. In M. M. Gruneberg, P. E. Morris, & R. N. Sykes (Eds.), *Practical aspects of memory* (pp. 84–92). London: Academic Press.

Crawford, C. B. (1994). *Strategic humor in leadership: Practical suggestions for appropriate use* (Report No. CS 508 544). Salina, KS: Kansas Leadership Forum. ERIC Document Reproduction Service No. ED 369 107).

Edworthy, A. (2000). *Managing stress*. Buckingham, Great Britain: Open University Press.

Goodman, J. (1983). How to get more smileage out of your life: Making sense of humor, then serving it. In P. E. McGhee, & J. H. Goldstein (Eds.), *Handbook of humor research, volume II, applied studies* (pp. 1–21). New York: Springer-Verlag.

Hobfoll, S. E. (1998). Stress, culture, and community: The psychology and philosophy of stress. New York: Plenum Press.

Johnson, P. R., & Indvik, J. (1990). The role communication plays in developing and reducing organizational stress and burnout. *Bulletin of the Association for Business Communications, 53*, 5–9.

Moody, R. A. (1978). *Laugh after laugh*. Jacksonville, FL: Headwaters Press.

Ziv, A. (1976). Facilitating effects of humor on creativity. *Journal of Educational Psychology, 68*, 318–322.

## Chapter 17

Barth, R. S. (1990). A personal vision of a good school. *Phi Delta Kappan, 71*, 512–516.

Blase, J. P., Dedrick, C., & Strathe, M. (1986). Leadership behavior of school principals in relation to teacher stress, satisfaction, and performance. *Journal of Humanistic Education and Development, 24*, 159–171.

Engelking, J. L. (1986). Teacher job satisfaction and dissatisfaction. *Spectrum, 4*, 1, 33–38.

Lane, W. (1993). Strategies for incorporating humor into the school climate. *Schools in the Middle, 2*, 4, 36–38.

Marlowe, J. (1995). The good, the bad, and the bozos. *Executive Educator, 17*, 9, 24–26.

Miller, B. J. (1991). *Dissatisfaction factors of Indiana home economics teachers* (Report No. CE 060 225). Los Angeles, CA: American Vocational Association. (ERIC Document Reproduction Service No. ED 341 779).

Nadeau, A., & Leighton, M. S. (1996). *The role of leadership in sustaining school reform: Voices from the field* (Report No. ED-ODS-96-2). Washington, DC: U.S. Department of Education. (ERIC Document Reproduction Service No. ED 399 643).

Pierson, P. R., & Bredeson, P. V. (1993). It's not just a laughing matter: School principals' use of humor in interpersonal communications with teachers. *Journal of School Leadership, 3*, 522–533.

Tishler, A. G., & Ernest, B. (1989). *Career dissatisfaction among Alabama teachers: A follow-up* (Report No. SP 031 916). Little Rock, AR: Mid-South Educational Research Association. (ERIC Document Reproduction Service No. ED 314 407).

Wilson, J. C. (1991). Making it in the big city. *Executive Educator, 13*, 9, 31–33.

Ziegler, V., & Boardman, G. (1986). Humor: The seventh sense in leadership. *National Forum of Educational Administration and Supervision, 2*, 2, 11–15.

Ziegler, V., Boardman, G., & Thomas, M. D. (1985). Humor, leadership, and school climate. *The Clearing House, 58*, 346–348.

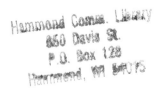